Anne Morrow Lindbergh

Anne Morrow Lindbergh

Between the Sea and the Stars

Beverly Gherman

Twenty-First Century Books • Minneapolis

For the Writers in My Life—Mentors All
Marilyn Sachs
Maxine Rose Schur
Susan Meyers
Gaby Rilleau
Andrea Stryer
Shirleyann Costigan
With Special Gratitude to Reeve Lindbergh
for her generous spirit

Twenty-First Century Books
A division of Lerner Publishing Group, Inc.
241 First Avenue North
Minneapolis, MN 55401 U.S.A.

Website address: www.lernerbooks.com

Library of Congress Cataloging-in-Publication Data

Gherman, Beverly.
    Anne Morrow Lindbergh : between the sea and the stars / by
Beverly Gherman.
        p.   cm.
    Includes bibliographical references and index.
    ISBN-13: 978–0–8225–5970–2 (lib. bdg. : alk. paper)
    ISBN-10: 0–8225–5970–6 (lib. bdg. : alk. paper)
    1. Lindbergh, Anne Morrow, 1906– 2. Authors, American—20th
century—Biography. 3. Air pilots—United States—Biography.
I. Title.
PS3523.I516Z66 2008
818'.5209—dc22   2005022498

Manufactured in the United States of America
1 2 3 4 5 6 – BP – 13 12 11 10 09 08

Contents

Anne Morrow was about three years of age when this photograph was taken.

ONE

Growing Up

I want to marry a hero.
—Anne Morrow Lindbergh, 1924

For Anne Morrow and her siblings, breakfast was always a rowdy beginning to the day. They beat their father, Dwight, to the table downstairs and were eating their cereal while their mother spread orange marmalade on the toast. Soon they heard Father upstairs whistling his same old song—always out of tune. He stomped down the stairs, still whistling. As soon as he reached the table, they all jumped up to kiss him. Sometimes they missed Father's cheek and ended up kissing one another.

Anne was born on June 22, 1906, the second daughter of Elizabeth and Dwight Morrow, a young lawyer. The family lived in Englewood, New Jersey, in a modest home surrounded by other small homes and other hardworking families. Anne's sister Elisabeth was two when Anne was born. Dwight Jr. was born in 1908 and then another sister, Constance (Con), in 1913.

Anne's mother,
Elizabeth Cutter Morrow

Elizabeth Morrow read to her children every afternoon at five o'clock. She read them *Heidi,* about a young girl who visits her grandfather in the high mountains of Switzerland. She also read them Louisa May Alcott's *Little Women,* about sisters growing up in New England who must help their mother when their father leaves to fight in the Civil War (1861–1865). Their father read them different fare, such as Rudyard Kipling's *Just So Stories* and *The Jungle Book* about a boy, Mowgli, and his adventures.

When the children were older, they read to themselves. Anne sometimes wrote in her diary or worked on her poetry. She also spent hours and hours writing letters to her grandmothers and to her family when they were apart.

Her parents spent summers in North Haven, Maine. They invited relatives to join them there. During the rest of the year, they all came together for Thanksgiving or Christmas in Englewood. The children enjoyed both sides of the family: Grandma Cutter and her daughters from Cleveland, Ohio, and the Morrows from Pittsburgh, Pennsylvania.

In 1910, when Anne was four, the family moved to a bigger house across town. The house was surrounded by an acre of land, including a handsome oak tree, a gum tree, and colorful gardens. Anne and her sister Elisabeth played for hours under the shade trees. Sometimes they pretended to be children lost in the forest. At other times, they were grand ladies traveling in coaches to visit royalty.

In 1911 the family began sailing to Europe on the ocean liners of the day. The Morrows thought the travel would help educate the children. They may have read about straight Roman roads, but Dwight wanted them to actually ride on those roads or see the aqueducts and temples the Romans built. Betty showed them where poets and novelists had lived.

Anne's father, Dwight Morrow

Anne at the age of nine had already traveled to Europe and the Bahama Islands.

They filled big steamer trunks with clothing, shoes, and hats for each of them. Even on board ship, they had to dress up for dinner every evening. They filled another trunk with books, from classics to thrillers, so that they were sure to find titles they liked. They made sure to include enough mysteries for their father.

Dwight gave up practicing law when he was asked to join the well-known banking institution, J. P. Morgan Company. He didn't look like most of the other Morgan officers. He was always rumpled and didn't care about outward appearances. But he was brilliant and honest.

Anne's mother became friendly with the other J. P. Morgan wives, and the Morrows began to take midwinter vacations in Nassau in the Bahama Islands with Morgan banking families. They stayed in a rented cottage there. It was a perfect time for Anne. She wrote and directed plays for all the children. She also spent time alone on the sandy beach, writing about the ocean and the beauty around her.

In 1919 the family moved to a New York City apartment on East Sixty-sixth Street. They returned to New Jersey only on the weekends. Thirteen-year-old Anne began school at Miss Chapin's School for Girls on nearby East 57th Street. The classes were small, and each girl was encouraged to develop her own talents. Anne's writing was free and fluid at school. She liked to experiment and turn ideas upside down. She wrote a fairy tale in which the dragon ate both the prince and princess because they were foolish and unworthy. Her story was published in the school's literary magazine the *Wheel*.

Anne was a good student, and she was elected president of the student council. She also played field hockey. The other girls appreciated her unassuming ways and made her a leader of their lively group.

With such varied interests and abilities, it would seem that Anne was a well-rounded, confident young girl. But she didn't feel confident. She called herself the "youngest, shyest, most self-conscious adolescent" who ever lived. She always put herself down and was afraid to ask for what she really wanted. But at her graduation dinner in 1924, when Miss Chapin asked the girls what their future goals were, Anne was not at all afraid to answer, "I want to marry a hero."

Anne's mother had gone to Smith College in Northhampton, Massachusetts. Her older sister, Elisabeth, was also attending Smith. Anne dreamed about going to Vassar instead. She had heard many of her classmates raving about New York's Vassar campus. She tried to explain in a letter to a friend : "I want to do something different." The letter ends, *"Of course* it would be hard and seem strange to everyone, but—oh gosh—I wish I *could!"*

Going to Vassar would allow her to be independent. She would not have to live in the shadow of her mother and sister. Elisabeth was popular with everyone, and she was also an excellent student. Anne didn't want that kind of pressure. She didn't want to be compared to her talented, beautiful sister all the time. But she knew it would hurt her mother if she broke the family tradition.

Despite her dream, Anne became a Smith student in September 1924. Her mother took her to school, unpacked her trunk, and hid some books under her pillow as a surprise.

There were 528 women in her freshman class. As a women's college, Smith always had encouraged young women to gain a strong sense of independence, despite the fact that most of the faculty was male. Anne found that Smith's president, William Neilson, was quite aware that women's roles were changing. The Neilsons were close friends of her mother, and they often invited Anne to their home and made sure she was comfortable on the campus.

Anne took classes in Greek, world history, psychology, music, and creative writing. She found that the writing class took up too much of her time because she wanted every page she wrote to be perfect. She complained that she was as slow as molasses and decided she would take English instead the following semester, because it would not require so much time. She knew that she had to live more fully so she would have meaningful experiences to write about.

In the fall of 1925, Anne sent her mother a poem she had written. She was so eager to know what her mother thought, she sent it overnight by special delivery instead of waiting several days for regular mail. She told her mother that the poem had just poured out of her and that felt so good because it had not happened for a long time.

Height

When I was young I felt so small
And frightened, for the world was tall.

And even grasses seemed to me
A forest of immensity,

Until I learned that I could grow
A glance would leave them far below.

Spanning a tree's height with my eye,
Suddenly I soared as high;

And fixing on a star I grew,
I pushed my head against the blue!

Still, like a singing lark, I find
Rapture to leave the grass behind.

And sometimes standing in a crowd
My lips are cool against a cloud.

The poem expresses her love of nature and her fear of life until she grows up and finds her place in the world. Even then, she was looking to the sky.

The Morrow children (left to right) *Elisabeth, Anne, Dwight Jr., and Constance appear in this studio portrait from the early 1920s.*

That spring she and three friends spent the day at the Sophia Smith Homestead, the house in which Smith College's founder lived. It had been restored with funds raised by Anne's mother. There they found the apple and cherry trees blanketed with pink and white blossoms. Below them were vast fields of violets and tall grass. Anne felt like sitting with her thoughts while her friends skipped and danced around and tried to get her to join them. She kept saying no. She wanted to be still. Later she wrote her mother how pleased she was to listen to herself and not be forced to follow someone else's wishes.

She also learned that she worked differently from other people. She took more time to think through her ideas. When she took her history exam, she was so slow she didn't even finish. She spent her time thinking and making notes before she started to write. There were three questions in the exam, and she hardly finished two. When the professor returned the exams, though, he read her answer aloud in class because she had approached one question well, even though her answer was incomplete.

When school let out, the whole family spent summers at their house in Maine along with friends and aunts and grandmothers. Anne saw that they were all happy to be together and thanked her Grandmother Cutter in a birthday letter for giving her mother the qualities that keep a family together and bring such joy. When her grandmother visited them in the summer, she taught them to do stitchery by pretending they were fine ladies who had come to tea. She showed them how to take tiny, neat stitches as they hemmed bureau covers and pincushion covers.

Anne went to Europe again with her family in the summer of 1926. A highlight of the trip was attending the opening of the League of Nations in Geneva, Switzerland, on September 6. It had been U. S. President Woodrow Wilson's dream that countries of the world would be able to solve their future disputes by talking rather than by war.

Afterward, Anne told one of her father's colleagues, who was the deputy secretary-general of the League, that she was not "educated enough" to attend the meeting. No, no, he protested. She had more education than some of the delegates.

By September Anne was eager to go home. She had had enough of fancy hotels and being waited upon. She wrote long, positive entries in her diary throughout the trip, but complained bitterly about having to live in such artificial settings as the Ritz Hotel.

She returned to Smith in the fall of 1926. "Caprice," a poem she wrote, was published in the literary journal, *Smith College Monthly,* that year. It begins:

Caprice

"I should like to be a dancer,
A slim persuasive dancer,
A scarlet Spanish dancer,
If you please!"...

There was room only for Quaker Maidens, she
was told.

So I play the role of Quaker
And I do not blame my maker
For I think I wear the Quaker
with a grace!

But when a tune is tilting,
Like a scarlet skirt is lilting,
That my rebel heart is lilting
No one sees.

Again, in this poem, Anne reveals her wish to be outgoing and livelier, very different from the quiet, controlled person she seemed to be.

In January 1927, she did poorly on exams. "I never never *never* work fast enough, really. I never finish, I never even get *enough done."* She received grades of a C and a B− even though she had been doing A work all through the year. She didn't seem to be able to function during exams or writtens (as they were then called), because she was so slow. She kept comparing herself to Elisabeth and how well she had done at Smith when she made dean's list and received honors in English. Dwight at Groton Preparatory School and Con at Milton Academy were at the head of their classes at school too.

Anne was asked to serve on the staff of the Smith literary magazine, the *Monthly.* She told her mother how happy she was, even though she was just a minor staff member and her mother had been the editor of the magazine. Her French teacher at Smith said of Anne's mother: "She is like some shooting star!" And again, Anne was reminded of her mother's success.

Dwight Morrow had been selected by President Calvin Coolidge to become ambassador to Mexico. The president thought Morrow would be skillful in improving economic relations between the two countries. In the fall of 1927, Anne began her senior year. Her mother visited her at Smith before she left with her husband and Con for Mexico on October 19.

Anne was tearful when she said good-bye to her mother. Mexico was so far away. They would not be able to share days as they had. But a few days later, she wrote her mother to say how happy she was for her parents to have this opportunity and that her mother should not worry about her tears.

TWO

A Special Hero

I can't treat him as an ordinary person (and will not treat him as an extraordinary one).
—Anne Morrow Lindbergh, 1927

In December of 1927, Anne and Elisabeth traveled by train from New York City to Mexico to be with the family for the holidays. In Texas Anne saw nothing but gray from the train window: gray cacti, low gray sagebrush, and beyond that a heavy gray sky. She found it desolate and depressing and wrote in her diary that she did not want to be stuck in such sad places, in such poor, small towns all across Texas.

As they entered Mexico, the landscape changed. It turned bright with sun and color. There were green trees, red berries, golden cornfields, blue and red houses, bright oranges and limes ripe on the branches. Anne wrote vivid descriptions of all she saw.

After three days on the train, Anne and Elisabeth arrived in Mexico City on December 21. Their parents and Con welcomed

For a publicity photo, Charles Lindbergh leans from the cockpit of the Spirit of St. Louis. *In this airplane, he became the first to successfully fly across the Atlantic Ocean from New York to Paris in 1927.*

them with big hugs and many questions. Then they squeezed into a car and drove to the embassy. On the way, her father told them that he had invited Charles Lindbergh to visit, thinking that the people of Mexico would welcome this young flier. He was famous everywhere in the world because he had flown alone nonstop from the United States to Paris, France, the previous May. He was the first person to make this amazing flight. Lindbergh had just flown to Mexico City nonstop from Washington, D.C., in the *Spirit of St. Louis,* the same plane that he had used in the transatlantic flight. Their father was certain they would like him.

Anne was disappointed. She wanted her family all to herself. She didn't care about Charles Lindbergh or his popularity or that the rest of the world adored him. If he was a flier, she assumed he couldn't be a reader. But he was already at the embassy, waiting for them. He had been there for almost a week.

That night an official embassy reception was held in Lindbergh's honor. Uniformed officers stood at attention along each side of the stairs. A red plush carpet led up the stairs to the porch where Charles Lindbergh stood waiting. Anne thought the whole scene ridiculous. Her mother introduced Colonel Lindbergh to her newly arrived daughters.

Anne later wrote in her diary, "I saw standing against the great stone pillar—on more red plush—a tall, slim boy in

Photographed during Christmas 1927 at the U.S. Embassy in Mexico City, this casual group includes (from left to right) Charles Lindbergh, Anne Morrow, her visiting cousin Richard Scandrett, and her sister Elisabeth.

evening dress—so much slimmer, so much taller, so much more poised than I expected. A very refined face, not at all like those grinning "Lindy" pictures—a firm mouth, clear, straight blue eyes, fair hair, and nice color. Then I went down the line, very confused and overwhelmed by it all. He did not smile— just bowed and shook hands."

After dinner the family and Colonel Lindbergh sat together in a small sitting room. Anne watched as Elisabeth asked Charles all sorts of questions, with ease. But she noticed that Charles answered her with short, blunt responses, as though he didn't seem at all comfortable.

When Con asked him if he liked the bullfight he had attended in Mexico, he answered curtly, "Well, I have seen things I enjoyed more." They asked to see the cape and sombrero he had been given at the bullfight. Awkwardly, he brought them back from his room and passed them around.

Anne began to feel some sympathy for him when he described the swarming crowds he had faced when he landed in Paris. She wrote in her diary, "And it was this *boy*—this shy, cool boy—and he describes that tremendous mad scene in a few dry matter-of-facts words."

Anne had not paid much attention to the famous Lindbergh flight. The newspapers had been filled with headlines and photos showing the huge welcome he had been given when he returned to the United States from Paris. There was a parade in Washington, D.C., and crowds of more than 250,000 people waited to see him. President Coolidge greeted Lindbergh, presented him with the Distinguished Flying Cross, and promoted him to colonel in the U.S. Army Air Reserve Corps. This was before the air force was established as a separate branch of the military. The post office issued a stamp with an image of his airplane, since it never issued stamps for living

Americans. He was famous throughout the world, no matter how stiff and awkward he seemed to Anne.

In a few days, it would be Christmas in Mexico. But outside it hardly seemed like winter. It was warm and sunny. That day they went to the airfield to greet Lindbergh's mother, who was flying in to be with Charles and the Morrow family for Christmas. Con told Anne that watching the large plane descend from the sky, with its five escort planes, was almost as exciting as watching Charles's arrival.

The crowd mobbed Evangeline Lindbergh as she stepped from the plane, but Dwight Morrow whisked her away, and they drove back to the embassy. Anne described her as a "small, sweet-faced, shy little woman" who seemed overwhelmed by so many strangers around her.

Later in the day, crowds surrounded the embassy. Anne was frightened by them. But she noticed that Charles seemed to be used to such mobs. She wondered if people were thrilled because of his amazing solo flight across the ocean. Or were they taken by this unassuming young man himself, so tall his head was above most of the people around him?

Charles seemed more and more uncomfortable around Anne and her sisters. She decided to avoid him, just as he was avoiding her. "I *can't* treat him as an ordinary person (and *will* not treat him as an extraordinary one)," she wrote in her diary.

On Christmas Day, she sat next to Charles for the midday meal in the enormous, high-ceiling dining room and tried to think of something interesting to say. Con asked him wonderful questions about flying. Anne was envious. Why couldn't she think of such good questions? Elisabeth also spoke to him easily about history and politics. Anne felt tongue-tied and awkward. Finally, she gathered her courage, leaned over to him, and confessed, "I'd almost always rather listen than talk." Charles didn't say a word, but he nodded his head as though he agreed completely.

Charles offered to take the family flying the next morning. He met them at the airfield next to the small silver plane that had brought his mother to Mexico City. He assisted everyone as they stepped up onto the wheel and into the plane. Charles took the front pilot's seat. He was dressed in a suit and a gray felt hat as though he were going to work. And as he bent to get into the plane, Anne realized it was true. He thought of flying as his work, as his whole life.

Charles started the engine and maneuvered the plane faster and faster along the ground until they lifted off. Soon they were in the sky, over the trees, the hangars, the fields, and the tiny embassy building. When she looked down, Anne could see the shadow of the plane as though it were a great bird. Below them the cars and people were tiny dots. Charles headed the plane toward the mountains. Anne loved the feeling of being in the air, being able to look down at the world and up at the blueness over their heads. She had no sense of fear, only a sense of freedom.

Charles made a large circle and then turned back toward the airfield. Soon he guided the plane down, landing it smoothly without a single jolt. Anne was so thrilled with the sensation of flying, she knew she had to fly again. Back at the embassy, the sisters talked with Charles about wanting to learn how to fly. He suggested different flight schools they might try. Anne could think of nothing else. "Clouds and stars and birds—I must have been walking with my head down looking at the puddles for twenty years," she wrote in her diary.

Back at school, she read everything she could find about Charles in magazines and newspapers. She filled her diary with lists of his personality traits. She thought he had "tremendous power over people," dignity, intelligence, sincerity, and good humor. She was discovering that a flier could be more interesting than she realized. But she knew that Charles liked Elisabeth better than he liked her. She had watched him listen to her sister's every word.

In January 1928, Anne returned to finish her last months at Smith. It didn't seem possible that the years had gone by so quickly. She felt she had become a different person from the one she had been when she first arrived. She was more outspoken and independent.

Anne worked hard in her classes, but she was still slow at writing exams and papers. Writing anything took her forever. Even so, that final semester she did well enough in her classes to make dean's list at last with a B+ average.

She kept thinking about what she would do with her life after she left school. She saw Charles Lindbergh living a meaningful life in the new field of aviation. She saw Elisabeth

Anne graduated from Smith at the age of twenty-two.

planning to open a school for young children. She wanted to find a way to make her own life important. She had learned that she was an observer. She noticed every detail in her surroundings. She hoped she would be able to use her observations and the things she loved in nature, in books, and in music to make a difference.

Now that she'd met him, Lindbergh fascinated her. She rushed to see the film, *Forty Thousand Miles with Colonel Lindbergh,* when it was shown in Northampton. She could hardly believe she knew the hero who was featured in it. She also read the many newspaper and magazine articles about him. According to them, he was twenty-six, eager to be out of the public eye, and ready to find a wife, although he claimed he still had not had a real date.

Anne learned that Charles was a shy, solitary child. He grew up in Little Falls, Minnesota, on a farm. When Charles was five, his father was elected to Congress and moved to Washington, D.C. Charles stayed in touch with him, but they never lived as a family again. Charles graduated from Little Falls High School in 1918, after spending the year working on a farm to help feed the troops in World War I (1914–1918).

Charles was intrigued by machinery and decided to study mechanical engineering at the University of Wisconsin in Madison. He bought a motorcycle and rode it to the university. After several semesters, he dropped out of school. His favorite class had been Reserve Officers' Training Corps (ROTC), where he learned to shoot a rifle and drill, but he didn't really concentrate on any of the other subjects.

He worked as a helper and mechanic for young men who were flying small planes and barnstorming, landing their planes in fields and offering airplane rides to local people. To attract attention, he did daredevil stunts such as walking on the wings of planes while they were in the air and parachuting from the cockpit. Charles became so skilled they called him Aerial Daredevil Lindbergh. He taught himself to fly and then enlisted in the army flying school, reporting to duty at Brooks Field in San Antonio, Texas. That's when he realized he had to work hard to pass classes in aerodynamics, navigation, and meteorology if he wanted to succeed.

Once he became a hero, reporters had followed his every move and even suggested names of women who would make a good wife. Anne knew she wasn't being considered as a possible spouse because she was still a student. She would have been thought too young for such a worldly man.

Crowds swarm around Charles's plane as he lands it in Paris on May 21, 1927. His famous flight across the Atlantic took 33.5 hours. After his feat, crowds formed around him wherever he went.

Her poem "Height" appeared in *Scribner's* magazine during her senior year. Instead of feeling thrilled, Anne was crit-
ical of her work. It was too sentimental, she thought. The line
about the lark made her "shudder!" when she reread it.

In early 1928, the family learned that Dwight Jr. seemed
to be suffering from a mental illness. He was hearing voices
and becoming agitated. He had to be hospitalized for
treatment.

Her mother returned to Englewood to be with Dwight Jr.
during his illness. In the spring, she went back to Mexico, and
Anne planned to spend her spring vacation there also, so they
took the train together. Elisabeth decided to stay in New Jersey with her brother.

Charles was still in her thoughts. Anne wrote Elisabeth
from the train, saying she was sure Colonel Lindbergh never
traveled by train. He didn't want to spend time in crowded
waiting rooms at train stations. And he didn't have to. He
could always fly.

She also wrote in her diary that "Colonel Lindbergh just
went ahead and did what he wanted terribly to do—what the
whole of him wanted sincerely and in a selfless kind of pas-
sion to do." She had just read about his heroic flight to Que-
bec, Canada, taking medicine to a pilot with pneumonia.

Anne was pleased to be with Con again in Mexico. They
were comfortable together, and neither of them worried about
what to say to each other. They had breakfast in the patio,
made sketches of the gate where the blue plumbago vine
trailed over the wall, and walked all over to see neighboring
gardens. All too quickly Anne's vacation was over, and she
had to return to school.

She and a friend drove to the airfield to see if a pilot
would take them flying. Soon a willing pilot helped them into

the plane, "twirled" (Anne's word) the propeller to start it, and jumped into his seat. They were flying!

They flew over the nearby hills and could see the land on both sides at once. The river looked like quicksilver; the houses, like toys. Anne and her friend were giddy with excitement when they landed. Afterward, whenever Anne was in her room and heard airplanes flying overhead, she felt the same thrill all over again.

In her diary, Anne described how when flying in the open cockpit, she felt "like God" looking at the fields, the hills, and the lakes—the natural world that seemed too beautiful to be real. Later, she tried to write poetry about how exquisite everything had been.

In the evenings, she daydreamed about Colonel Lindbergh and wondered whether he liked her. Then she wondered whether she might win the Jordan Literary Prize for a paper she had written. She went back and forth in her thoughts. Colonel Lindbergh never even looked at her. How could he like her? She didn't deserve a prize.

Then she did win the Jordan Literary Prize and a prize for the best essay on eighteenth-century women. Her paper told the story of Madame d'Houdetot, a friend of the French writer and philosopher Jean-Jacques Rousseau. For the Jordan Literary Prize, she had written a story called "Lida Was Beautiful." In it her character envies a cousin who is beautiful and feels sorry for herself because she is plain. Her mother was ecstatic to learn that she had won two prizes.

By June 22, Anne was in North Haven, Maine, staying in the large, new house her parents had built at Deacon Brown's Point. She was glad to have the chance to spend time with Con again.

Thoughts about Charles still consumed her. She described him as the "finest man I have ever met...and someone utterly opposite to me. So opposite that I don't exist at all for him or in his world." In July she learned that Lindbergh was not coming to Maine to see the family. Instead, he was going to see Elisabeth in New York. Anne tried to accept the fact that he was the right partner for her sister.

She told her diary, "I want to be married, but I never, never will." Even though she described meeting pleasant young men who seemed to like her, she didn't like them well enough to consider them for marriage. She was comparing all of them to the tall, young flier she had met in Mexico.

THREE

High as the Sky

*He opened the door to 'real
life' and although it frightened
me, it also beckoned.*
—Anne Morrow Lindbergh, 1924

In the fall of 1928, Charles called the Englewood house
to speak to the Morrows or to Elisabeth. Mrs. Morrow's secretary Jo answered the phone. She told him they were not living at the house right then. But Anne was, Jo said, and she
would be home later that evening. Colonel Lindbergh said he
would call again the next day, around ten in the morning to
speak to her.

Anne could hardly sleep that night thinking about his
phone call. In the morning, the phone rang on the dot of ten.
She just sat there looking at it, letting it ring, wondering how
she would be able to say a word. Finally, she said a quiet,
"Hello." He also answered quietly, "Hello. This is . . . Lindbergh himself." She asked him how he was, and he answered
formally, as though he were reading from notes.

30

"When I was south last winter I promised to take you up sometime here in the east," he said. "I called up to tell you I'd be very glad to arrange a flight, if you'd care to go."

Anne was shocked, but she told him she would love to go, except that she wouldn't be able to get away for at least a week, and he would probably be too busy then. But he wasn't too busy, he said. He would call her the following week.

Charles Lindbergh called promptly at ten on Wednesday morning, exactly a week later. Jo told him she would be home that evening. Charles called back in the evening, saying, "Hello, this is Lindbergh speaking." He suggested he come out to the house the next day around four o'clock to talk about the flight. He was certainly keeping his word, but Anne was sure he was "doing it out of duty" to thank her father.

The next day, she sat outside waiting for him, looking at her favorite pair of trees in the garden. The "married ones," she called them, because the big oak was tall and protective

Charles filled Anne's thoughts as 1928 drew to a close.

of the shorter, lacy tree. Checking her watch, she saw that Charles was late. It was already after four o'clock. The later he was, the more determined Anne was to act aloof when he arrived.

Charles finally arrived. He was embarrassed and upset that he had been late. He followed her into the house, sat right down, and began asking her questions about their flight. Where should they go, in what kind of plane? He explained that they had to be careful not to be seen together or the newspapers would have them engaged the next day. Anne tried to look sorry for him.

He asked where Elisabeth was, whether she would soon be in Mexico, and what Con was doing. Anne told him that Elisabeth was in Europe and that Con was writing a paper about aviation. She should be the one to go flying, Anne said. He was pleased and said he would take her flying too.

Anne found the whole visit difficult. She told Con that he was "cold—he is the coolest man I've ever met" and that it was quite obvious he wanted to see Elisabeth and was taking her only because he had to. The day of the flight finally came, Tuesday, October 16. Charles picked her up in New York City, at an apartment belonging to friends of her parents. He drove his new sleek car, a Franklin sedan, to the Long Island estate of Harry Guggenheim, a wealthy promoter of aviation, and his wife, Carol. They would have lunch there before the flight.

Anne talked about the three times she had flown in Northampton and told him that she had never told her parents, so he must keep her secret. He wondered what she was going to do now that she had finished school. She said she'd thought of teaching but didn't think she was "quick enough." They talked about flying over Mexico, which he loved.

By the time they reached Falaise, the Guggenheim estate, Anne felt quite comfortable with him. She had stopped feeling afraid of him and thought he "was *terribly* kind and absolutely natural. . . . He's rather a dear," she wrote to Con, completely reversing her previous opinion. She had forgotten how very tall he was, she told her sister.

Charles had lived with Harry and Carol Guggenheim when he was writing his autobiography, *We*—meaning Charles and the group of supporters who sponsored his flight to Paris. He felt right at home with the Guggenheims. For years Harry had been using his family's great wealth to develop safe commercial flight. Charles was helping him to achieve this dream.

Anne had never met the Guggenheims, but she found lunch an eye-opener as they shared many of Charles' practical jokes. They told about how, in flight school, Charles (they nicknamed him "Slim") had played tricks on the other men. He had put shaving cream in one sleeping fellow's open mouth, turned the hose on another sleeper, and hid a third fellow's gear on the roof.

After lunch Charles went to the nearby Roosevelt Field to get the rented plane, a De Havilland Gipsy Moth biplane, with its two open cockpits and double wings. He landed it on the field

The biplane Charles rented for his flight with Anne in the fall of 1928 would have looked like this DH.60G De Havilland Gipsy Moth but would not have had pontoons for water landings.

behind the Guggenheim estate. It was lightweight and didn't need much space for landing and taking off.

Thinking she needed to dress warmly, Anne had worn a pair of Con's horseback riding pants, a heavy red leather jacket, and her father's thick golf stockings, but she also wore one of her fashionable hats and high-heeled shoes. Charles told her to take off her hat and handed her a brown helmet and goggles. He insisted she put on a parachute in case she needed it, and he said she should have worn boots.

He helped her as she climbed into the plane by stepping up onto the tire. Then he showed her how to work the wooden rudders with her feet to keep the plane level. He also showed her how the control stick would lift the plane's nose or lower it. When they were aloft, he signaled for her to take the stick. She had trouble moving it because the winds were strong, but she tried anyway. "Flying . . . was too glorious," she later wrote Con.

On the drive back in his car, Charles confessed how difficult it was for him to talk to strangers, especially to answer their silly questions. Anne admitted she was shy with people too, but she didn't have to deal with crowds as he did. She told him that those large mobs of people in Mexico had frightened her. He responded with a smile, "If ever you get into a crowd and they start mauling you, just kick their shins—they don't know who's doing it!"

Later that week, Charles took Anne up again to fly over New York City and New Jersey, landing back on Long Island. This time the papers got wind of the trip, assumed it was Elisabeth flying with Charles, and printed headlines, saying "Lone Eagle No Longer Lonely—Courts Elisabeth Morrow." The Lone Eagle was a nickname he acquired after his solo flight to France.

Anne's father had said earlier that they were to have nothing to do with Charles Lindbergh if there should be any publicity. And there it was. Charles came to supper at the house and laughed about the headlines. He had been "engaged" to several young women in the newspapers, even ones that he had never met, so he told her it was nothing to worry about. He hoped her father wouldn't prevent him from seeing Anne and her sisters.

After dinner, he took Anne driving and they found new things to talk about. He wondered what Anne's family first thought of him when they met him in Mexico. She told him they thought he was the "stern Norse god," and that she was really afraid of him then. He agreed that he might be stern, but Anne quickly told him he was also "very kind."

They talked about what they would do with their lives. He knew he wanted to link countries of the world through his flying. He thought it would help destroy people's prejudices about one another. She confided that she wanted to write and that she also wanted to learn to fly. He encouraged her in her writing and her plan to fly. By the time he took her home, he had asked her to marry him.

"You must be kidding!" Anne said. "You don't know me." But Charles insisted that he did know her. He could see that she was adventurous and appreciative of nature, that she would be a perfect partner for his flying career and his life. Anne could hardly believe this was happening. But she said yes, she would marry him. They agreed to keep it a secret, even from her siblings and her parents.

On her way to the Mexican embassy in late October, Anne wrote Elisabeth using a false name for Charles, "Great God Boyd," a name that had been used in a magazine story about a young flier, obviously based on Lindbergh. Elisabeth was recuperating in England after a serious case of pneumonia. Anne told her how "Boyd" had called to speak with Elisabeth about a flying trip but had to take Anne, the ugly duckling, instead.

Anne did not let on that Charles had asked her to marry him. "He is really quite a dear!" she told Elisabeth. She didn't tell anyone that she was worried about their differences, about what she saw as the "hideous chasm" between them.

When they were together, she had told him about the literature she loved: the poets, the authors who expressed their honest feelings in their writing. She thought many modern writers did not do this well. But she knew that he didn't share her love for books and rarely even opened a book unless it was about aviation.

Anne settled in the embassy in Mexico and waited. Charles flew in on November 19. That evening they went to a dinner dance with a few other friends. All the young girls swamped Charles, asking him silly questions and batting their eyes at him.

In the morning, Anne and Charles drove down to Cuernavaca to spend a few days with her family at the house the Morrows were renovating for a weekend home. She and Charles tried to talk in the courtyard, but workers were everywhere, inside and outside the house.

A few days later, when all was quiet, Charles asked the Morrows to join him in the courtyard. He said he wanted to share his thoughts with them. He told them that he wanted to marry Anne, and he hoped they would approve. Her parents were astounded. Her mother, especially, worried that Charles and Anne were too different and that they hardly knew each other. But she thought that Anne loved him.

Her father walked around mumbling that it was too soon, and they hardly knew anything about Charles, even though he had been the one to invite Charles to the embassy. The three of them agreed to keep it a secret until Charles told them it was all right to make a formal announcement.

All of them returned to the embassy on Monday. Charles took Anne flying in a Curtiss Falcon, another biplane, with two cockpits and dual controls. By waving his hands above his head, he signaled her to take control of the plane. When she did, she discovered she could fly the plane much better than she had in New York. He let her fly until they came close to the volcanic mountains. She was glad to let him take over again, so that she could watch as the plane rose over the straight green firs. She saw where the tree line ended and the lava flow began. There were snow-covered rocks and then an enormous crater left from an earlier eruption. When they passed over a smaller crater, she could see that people had planted corn inside it.

Charles stayed in Mexico for two weeks. He and Anne spent a great deal of time together. She wrote her sister Con that Charles was like the sun and she felt it was blinding to be with him. Other people talk about him as the great hero, she wrote, but she was finding it difficult to "reconcile *that person* with the one we know."

Anne was in love with him, although she still had questions about the differences between them. At meals Charles was silent, not needing to talk all the time, while the others were sharing ideas and discussing issues. A friend described Charles as "that Viking Silence."

Anne wrote Elisabeth, who had returned to the United States and was staying with friends on Long Island. Elisabeth was still quite weak after her pneumonia. Anne told her about the two weeks she had spent with Charles. She wrote: "He is terribly young and crude in many small ways (the books he's read, and liking to play tricks) and quite seerlike in tremendous outlooks."

She continued, "As you can see, I am completely turned upside down, completely overwhelmed, completely upset. He is the biggest, most absorbing person I've ever met, and he doesn't seem to touch my life anywhere, really."

She wrote Con that she had been confused and immobilized ever since he left. She heard her friends making fun of him, of "his lack of sense of humor, his practical jokes, his one-track mind." Certainly they were right, but now that she knew him better, she realized he had many positive qualities that others did not recognize.

As close as she was to her sisters, she still didn't tell them that she and Charles had agreed to marry. But by writing them about her concerns, she was almost talking to herself and working out her feelings.

Back in Englewood, Anne had to pack up her belongings and say a sad good-bye to the house where they had grown up. The family was moving to an enormous new home in Englewood, called Next Day Hill, with more than fifty acres of land and gardens surrounding it. A large staff would be required to care for its grounds and many rooms. She wrote Elisabeth about how she visited the old house, remembering all they had done or seen in each space: the room they shared that had the blue roses screen; the guest room where they stayed when one of them had the measles; Mother's bedroom where they sat on the green sofa to hear Bible stories; and Dwight's room where they sat and read to him when he was ill. In the garden, where they had played, she looked at all the bushes and trees and said good-bye to the married pair.

Before the end of the year, Anne told her siblings that she was to marry Charles. Then she confided in her old friend Corliss Lamont, who had lived nearby and who had grown up with her. She knew that Corliss would be quite surprised that she had chosen "the great Western strong-man-open-spaces type and a life of relentless action!" He was exactly opposite of what she

An aerial view of Next Day Hill

always said she would choose—a man who shared everything she loved and who wanted the same quiet life she did.

She told Corliss not to wish her happiness. "Wish me courage and strength and a sense of humor—I will need them all." She ended her letter with thoughts about Charles: "He has vision and a sense of humor and extraordinarily nice eyes!"

For several months, Anne weighed the positives and negatives of marrying Charles as carefully as she'd answered questions on her exams at Smith. She was torn between the great love she felt for him and her concern that she and Charles shared few interests.

What finally convinced her was that Charles understood her need to rebel from her conventional life. Life with him promised the adventures she craved. "The sheer fact of finding myself loved was unbelievable and changed my world, my feeling about life and myself," Anne wrote many years later to explain her decision. "He opened the door to 'real life' and although it frightened me, it also beckoned. I had to go."

Early in 1929, at the age of twenty-two, Anne told Charles she did love him and wanted to marry him, even though they were extremely different people. She wrote her sister Con, "I am sure *sure sure* that it is right now, and the pangs are not doubt any more."

Soon it was no longer a secret that Anne and Charles would be married. On February 12, Ambassador Morrow told journalists in Mexico City that Charles and Anne were engaged. He was besieged by questions. When will they marry? Where? How do you feel about it? He told the reporters he had nothing more to say.

Anne and Charles avoided the press so they would not have to answer any questions either. Anne received hundreds of congratulatory letters from her friends, her family's friends, and from people she didn't even know.

"L to Wed Anne S. Morrow," read one of the newspaper headlines. The papers often included a photograph of Charles and the Morrows with their daughter Con, rather than Anne.

Journalists kept watch over the embassy in Mexico and the Morrows' new houses in Maine and in Englewood, hoping to see preparations for the wedding. They tried to get information from the Morrow staff or from their friends. When that didn't work, they had to stake out all three sites themselves.

Anne stayed in Mexico with her parents while Charles left to fly new mail routes in Latin America for Pan American Airways. He had told her not to write to him. Think about what would happen if the newspapers were to find her letters, he had said. Her words would end up in their headlines. But she could not stop writing. It was her life. She continued to write in her diary and to wish that she could send him letters about her feelings. She read about his travels in the newspapers, but received nothing from him. After weeks of not hearing from him, she grew resentful.

Finally, Charles joined her at the family's weekend home in Cuernavaca. He and Anne decided to fly out of the city to a deserted area where they could picnic and be alone.

On the way back, Charles signaled Anne that a wheel had fallen off the plane. He told her to open her window, and he handed her a thick flying suit to put on and a cushion to protect her if the plane flipped over on landing. He flew around for almost two hours to use up the gasoline, which might explode on impact. Anne tried to look at the beauty around her and not panic. Finally, Charles signaled he was going to land.

Anne saw a crowd of people waiting for them. She later said they'd looked like "little ants down there below us." The

Charles (right) *worked for Pan American Airways. While engaged to Anne, he flew new mail routes in South America.*

people pointed at the missing wheel and signaled that they should not land. "It really was dramatic," she later wrote. "We looked at each other and laughed and circled the field again." She had "one terrible moment of panic: Now here is the test," she told herself. "Suppose you can't face it. You will just be ruined in his eyes." Anne knew she had to act bravely. She told herself to keep her eyes open, not to cry, not to think about crashing. She concentrated on watching Charles. He would bring them down safely.

Before she knew it, Charles landed the plane on its good wheel, and the force turned them over. But "it wasn't so terrible," she later wrote to Con. Anne was able to climb through the window, shaken but unhurt. Charles was not so lucky. He had dislocated his right shoulder as he grasped the fuselage during the landing.

Climbing out of the damaged plane, he faced the crowd, trying not to show his pain. He told them it was a minor incident and that they were both fine. They would be flying again in just a few days, he reassured them. Then the reporters shouted questions for Anne. She was not yet ready to face them on her own. Instead, she began her new life by letting Charles speak for her.

FOUR

Marriage

*We were unable to lead our
private lives without
being hounded. . . .*
—Anne Morrow Lindbergh, 1980

The Morrows wanted to plan Anne and Charles's wedding while they were all together in Mexico. Her mother made a long guest list and assumed the wedding would be held in the Englewood Presbyterian Church. Anne and Charles had different ideas. They wanted a small wedding, perhaps at the Maine house, certainly not in a church where crowds could surround them and intrude on their happiness.

After Charles left on March 14, Anne began writing letters to him describing her love of literature and the way she looked at life, hoping she could influence him to share her feelings. She had to tell him how much she loved him and missed being with him, even though he had told her not to.

But just in case anyone did see her letters, she was careful not to mention a word about their decision to marry at the end

43

of May. The family left Mexico City a month before the wedding date. Elisabeth and Anne spent time together in Englewood planning details of the wedding.

Anne's brother, Dwight, was still not well enough to leave the hospital in Stockbridge, Massachusetts, where he had been getting treatment for his illness, which had been diagnosed as schizophrenia. But the rest of the family and Charles's mother would be there. The plan was to have a large party in Englewood the day before the wedding. It would be a celebration for Betty Morrow's fifty-fourth birthday. In order to deceive the reporters, Charles had serviced his airplane and stored it in the hangar at Roosevelt Field in New York. That's where the reporters camped out, waiting for Lindbergh and his bride to leave on their honeymoon.

Meanwhile, a small group of family and close friends had been invited for tea on Monday, May 27, 1929, the day after the birthday party. They had no idea there was to be a wedding that afternoon.

In the morning, Anne cut flowers from the new gardens to beautify the house. She also went back to the old house on Palisade Avenue to gather some from its garden. Elisabeth made a small bouquet for Anne to carry down the aisle. They all had a light lunch with Charles' mother and the aunts, and then Anne and Charles drove off, once again trying to deceive the small group of reporters outside.

The guests began to arrive around four o'clock. Altogether, there were twenty-two people. Betty thought her daughter looked "like a vision" in a long, cream-colored gown and French lace veil. Charles wore a blue suit. He stood tall, and Anne barely reached his shoulder.

The service was exactly what Anne and Charles had chosen. They stood in front of the fireplace in the living room where the minister spoke their vows with them. No one took a photograph to record the moment.

A neighbor had smuggled in a wedding cake the day before. Betty thought the frosting was hard as a rock and the punch tasted awful, but none of that mattered to the young couple. Anne and Charles were happy to be surrounded by their families. He told Anne that he loved their wedding, but the best part was "the family, the whole family, and nothing but the family." They changed into casual clothes and again drove off, waving to the reporters.

Later that evening, a friend of Anne's father came out and told the small group of waiting reporters that Anne and Charles had been married earlier in the day. That was all the information he would share.

The newlyweds were already on a motorboat, called *Mouette*—French for "seagull"—cruising along the New England coast. Charles had filled the pantry with very unusual foods, cans of pâté, shrimp, plum pudding, and baked beans.

He assumed that Anne would take care of the meals and the boat's cleanliness, while he would be the captain at the wheel. Anne had mixed feelings about the division of duties and about all the work Charles expected her to do. Sometimes, she wrote, she felt as if they had gone camping and she was his assistant, not his partner.

She had packed books to read, and one morning she made him sit and listen as she read poetry, thinking she could persuade him to enjoy works she loved. "He was bored to tears," she realized, but he found a romantic poem by A. E. Housman in her collection, and he read it aloud to her to prove that he could appreciate poetry too.

She began a long, continuous letter to her mother telling her all of the amusing things that happened to them. How Charles had gone on land, disguised by his growing beard, dark glasses, and a cap pulled over his eyes. He went to get more water, and when the local fishermen asked about his fancy boat, he told them he was Charles Lindbergh. Hiding behind the curtains below ship, Anne heard the men laugh in disbelief. Sure, he was Lindbergh! they scoffed.

They made it up to the coast of Maine before being discovered. They were able to elude boats filled with reporters when they headed away from land. As a wedding present, Anne's father had given them a small island, called Big Garden, near North Haven. They found it on the map and visited the wild island before they turned back.

On their return to New York, they stayed at the Berkshire Hotel in Manhattan, where they were recognized by the staff and some of the other guests staying on the same floor. The attention was a constant reminder for Anne that her life would never be the same. She and Charles would be followed as celebrities no matter where they went.

Anne walks the coast of Maine on her honeymoon with Charles in June 1929.

In her diary, Anne expressed her concern about what her life would be like. "Life in the air was beautiful, limitless, and free—if often hazardous—but life on the ground married to a public hero was a full-cry race between hunter and hunted. We were the quarry. We were unable to lead our private lives without being hounded."

From the hotel, Anne wrote her brother, Dwight, about all that she had learned on the boat, including how to use a compass. She thought she was becoming a good sailor and ship's mate, she told him. She and Charles hoped he would go with them on a boat trip soon.

Several weeks later, Charles began flying for TAT (Transcontinental Air Transport) airlines to inaugurate new routes, and he wanted Anne to join him. They flew in an open Curtiss Falcon biplane through New Jersey, Pennsylvania, Ohio, and Indiana. She saw how crowds adored her husband everywhere they stopped. She had to learn to deal with the people they met at every stop while being careful not to say anything personal. It didn't seem to matter what either of them actually said. The newspapers made up stories about them everywhere they went.

Anne's love for flying grew with each flight. She captured in her diary what she was seeing and feeling. She described cities viewed from above as squares of "wet earth" she could almost smell. She wrote about the brilliance of a rainbow at sunset. The couple continued on to New Mexico, where they photographed ruins of early Native American cities that had been seen only from the air. In a letter to her mother, Anne described all these sights and thanked her for what she had said when she first heard that Anne and Charles would marry: "Anne, you'll have the sky—the sky!

Anne learned to fly and received her student pilot license in August 1929.

FIVE

Flying Solo

*[I was] challenged, frightened,
and infuriated trying to satisfy
my exacting instructor.*
—Anne Morrow Lindbergh, 1973

It wasn't enough for Anne to take the controls while she and Charles flew. She wanted to learn to fly on her own. Charles began to give her lessons so that she could get her student pilot's license. They drove from Englewood to the Aviation Club on Long Island. After nine hours of flying together with dual controls, Anne was ready to take her solo flight in late August.

Confidently, she took off by herself in the plane, rose five hundred feet in the air, circled the field, and landed. She repeated this two more times, each time going slightly higher and circling wider. Charles waited for her on the porch of the aviation club, beaming with pride at how well his student was doing.

He had been a demanding teacher, making her repeat each landing until she was able to touch the ground perfectly, without a single bump. Anne wrote she was "challenged, frightened, and infuriated trying to satisfy my exacting instructor."

She and Charles continued to fly for TAT, stopping every day in a different small town across the Midwest. They were even invited by President and Mrs. Hoover to spend some time at the White House and at the outdoor camp the Hoovers loved. Next, they stopped to see Anne's Grandma Cutter in Cleveland and Charles's mother and his Uncle Charles in Detroit. Anne was fond of Charles's mother. "She is really wonderful . . . . I love her quick, sharp Irish wit," she wrote Elisabeth.

At last they joined the Morrows in Maine for a few days in September. The house at North Haven was large and comfortable, and Anne was happy to be back with her parents and Con. Now that they were all grown up, she adored having sisters and told Charles how lucky she felt being able to share every event or thought with them.

On September 18, she and Charles left again for another long flight over the Caribbean to South and Central America. They made stops every day and sometimes several times a day, but Anne was still not used to the crowds and the questions people asked. "I have no patience, no understanding, no sympathy with the people who stare and follow and giggle at us," Anne wrote.

By October they were back in the United States, and Anne was feeling nauseated. She hoped that meant she was pregnant. The doctor confirmed it, and Charles agreed to wait to travel west to Los Angeles, California, until she was feeling better. He was going there to pick up his new airplane, a Lockheed Sirius seaplane with two closed cockpits. He had requested dual controls, so that either of them could fly the plane on their own. There would be a sliding canopy over the two cockpits and a generator to keep their flying suits warm. But most important,

Charles (left) *and Anne land their new Lockheed Sirius seaplane.*

the plane could land on water and would include a long-range radio, which Anne would operate.

They left for the West Coast at the end of the year. Anne rested at the end of every day, memorizing poetry that she could recite when they were flying. She found there were sad poems and happy poems, but none that dealt with the true emotion of flying that "get you around the throat."

Anne wrote her family the happy news that she was expecting a baby and told them how thrilled she and Charles were. She asked them not to say a word to anyone else. She also wrote Charles's mother, asking her to keep their wonderful secret.

In January 1930, in California, Charles began teaching Anne how to operate a glider plane, a plane without an engine that rode on the winds. He suggested she take her glider pilot's test and chose a mountain peak, Soledad, in San Diego, California for her final test. She said that gliders reminded her of kites

Hawley Bowlus [standing left] trained both Anne [right] and Charles [behind Bowlus] for the glider pilot's license test.

being towed behind a car until they rise at least five hundred feet in the air and are then released.

Anne was "frightened to death" as an airplane pulled her glider from the peak, but she didn't want to show her fear to Charles, who always seemed fearless. Once the plane released the glider though, she found she was delighted with the silence, the overwhelming quiet surrounding her. She adjusted the glider to meet air currents that lifted the plane, and then the currents dropped it down, down, down slowly and gently into a meadow at the bottom of the mountain, where she landed easily on the ground.

Startled drivers and people in nearby houses came running to see what had fallen from the mountain. Anne had been in the air for the six required minutes and would get her license. She became the first licensed woman glider pilot in the United States and a charter member of the girls' glider clubs that formed everywhere.

Charles's new plane was ready by the end of April. He and Anne planned to fly the Sirius back to New York. Anne was seven months pregnant, and Charles had made a small ladder so that she could climb into the plane more easily. They left Los Angeles, made a single stop in Wichita, Kansas, for fuel, and landed in New York almost fifteen hours later. They had broken the previous flying record by almost three hours. Charles had decided to fly higher and carry less fuel in order to make time. Thousands of people were waiting to greet them at the airport.

Anne had been suffering from a severe headache and nausea for the last few hours of the trip, but she didn't want to tell Charles because she knew he was eager to set a record. If he had known, he might have stopped the flight. Once they were on the ground, she had to be helped out of the plane. Her body had been crammed into the small cockpit for too many hours, and she could hardly walk after they landed. Years later, she admitted that it had not been a good idea to fly so late in her pregnancy.

Anne and Charles moved into Next Day Hill in Englewood to wait for the baby's birth. At that time, the house was almost a medical clinic. Doctors were coming to see Elisabeth, who was recovering at home from a heart attack. She and a friend had opened a nursery school called the Little School. It had forty young children under the age of six. All the effort Elisabeth made to get the school ready had been too much for her. It was then that the family learned that she had a damaged heart valve from the rheumatic fever she'd had as a child. In those years, medicine could do little to heal her condition.

Their brother, Dwight, was also home, and his doctor came frequently to see him. Fortunately, there were enough rooms in the house and enough staff to care for the extra family.

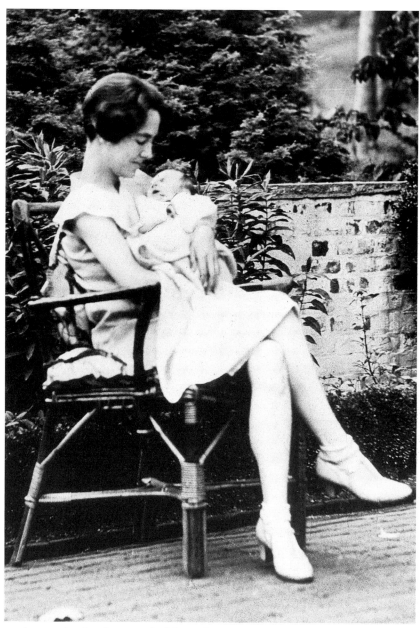

Anne sits in the sun holding Charles Lindbergh Jr.

SIX

Baby Charles

*So self-controlled, so calm,
so factual, in the midst of
horror and suspense?*
—Anne Morrow Lindbergh, 1973

When Anne was ready to deliver the baby, nurses and doctors came to the house to assist her. Charles held Anne's hand during the eleven-hour labor. The baby was born on Anne's twenty-fourth birthday, on June 22, 1930. Charles telegraphed his mother, using a special code they had worked out to tell her Anne had given birth to a son. His telegram read: "advising purchasing property." If the baby had been a girl, it would have read: "advising accepting terms of contract."

Charles waited two weeks before holding a press conference to give details about the baby. He told them that his son was named Charles Augustus Lindbergh Jr., and he passed out a picture he had taken of the newborn. People all over the country sent cards, poems, and gifts. Some others, annoyed by the constant Lindbergh news, wrote angry letters to the news media for continuing stories about the famous family.

Anne wrote her mother-in-law that she was disappointed because she thought the baby looked like her, but then she discovered that he had Charles's mouth and the "unmistakable cleft in the chin!" Soon the baby was gaining weight and beginning to smile the same wide smile that Charles had. His eyes were deep blue.

In the 1930s, books about the philosophy of child care told parents not to handle or cuddle their babies too much. One expert, Dr. John Watson, wrote "Never hug and kiss them, never let them sit on your lap. If you must, kiss them once on the forehead when you say good night." Anne thought his ideas were silly, but she found she didn't have a desire to cuddle the baby or hold him more than necessary, although she loved talking to him and watching him respond. She bathed him, dressed him, and gave him his bottles, but she was pleased to have hired Betty Gow, a competent nurse, so that she could feel safe about leaving him when she had to.

In September 1930, the Lindberghs rented an old farmhouse close to Princeton, in Hopewell, New Jersey. They also bought land nearby with a hill and a brook and lovely old oaks, planning to build their own home there. They would call it High Fields.

After they moved into the farmhouse, they discovered six tiny ducklings and eggs the chickens had laid in the nearby gardens. Anne liked the quiet, rural setting. She planted tulip and crocus bulbs, looking forward to their colors, come spring. Baby Charles was getting so plump that Anne called him "my fat lamb." He took his nap in the barn and loved it when Charles took him "ceiling flying" in his arms.

Anne also hired a British couple, Oliver and Elsie Whateley, to care for the house and the grounds. Those early months in the Princeton farmhouse were happy ones.

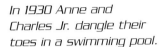

In 1930 Anne and
Charles Jr. dangle their
toes in a swimming pool.

Charles went into New York frequently to work with Dr. Alexis Carrel at the Rockefeller Institute for Medical Research. They were doing research on replacing defective heart valves with mechanical valves made in the laboratory. Charles's initial interest was to help Elisabeth, who was growing weaker because of the diseased valve in her heart.

Charles was also planning a survey flight for the airlines. He was going west through Canada, Alaska, and Siberia to Japan and China. In preparation for the long flight, Charles wanted Anne to get her final pilot's license, in case he needed her to take over the plane. The student license she already had was not enough—especially because they would be flying in their Lockheed Sirius, which landed on water as well as on land.

Anne wrote Charles's mother about the new round of flying lessons. "Some good days, some bad days, some scoldings, etc.

You know the way it is." Charles was exacting, expecting her to do everything perfectly. She found it difficult to meet his high standards and felt frightened and worried every time she took off. "I remember going round and round the field alone in that plane, making one hideously bumpy landing after another," she wrote. She was glad to be down, no matter how bumpy her landing, but Charles insisted she go up again and make a better one. That's how he perfected his flying— by repeating every move until it couldn't be done better.

Each time she landed, she did improve until she had mastered the technique. At last she was confident enough to make solo flights over New York City.

She received her pilot's license on May 30, after flying solo for the required ten hours. She made four perfect landings, spiraled from two thousand feet, and did figure eights. On the ground, she spent long hours studying radio theory, as well as the dots and dashes of Morse code, so that she could operate the radio on their plane.

Anne was nervous about leaving baby Charlie, but she was reassured when her mother offered to care for him at North Haven, where the family would spend the summer. At the end of July, Betty Gow and Charlie left first, taking a train to North Haven. Anne and Charles flew to Maine to say good-bye to them and to the rest of her family on July 29, 1931. The next day, they flew to Ottawa, Canada, then north to a place called Moose Factory. There were Native Americans living there and some men from the Hudson's Bay Company, a company that had been operating trading posts in that area since 1650.

As they continued north to Churchill in Manitoba on Hudson Bay, Anne wrote her mother that the north star seemed to be on top of them, guiding their way, and that they had just seen the most beautiful northern lights in the evening sky for the first time.

Many of the men they met were fur trappers who had been in Churchill for as long as six years without leaving. They all asked questions about the "outside" world. Native people lived there too, but no white woman had visited this isolated area before. Anne felt they were disappointed with her because she was wearing trousers and didn't look at all feminine.

They spent three days at Barrow, Alaska, and Anne was touched by the generosity of the native people, who lent her sealskin boots to keep her feet dry and showed her safe places to walk on the ice and snow.

Anne (center) and Charles (second from right) are dressed for the cold weather in Barrow, Alaska, in August 1931.

The chief radio officer at Nemuro, Japan, confers with Anne who operated the radio on the flight to Japan in August 1931.

They flew on to Osaka, Japan, and then to Tokyo, where large crowds came out to greet them. It was already September, and Anne had expected to be home with Charlie by then. She missed him terribly. She wrote her mother-in-law that she was not happy being away from him so long, but she dare not make a fuss because Charles would not like it. She wrote her mother that she dreamed about Charlie every night.

When they landed in Nanjing, China, the Chang, or Yangtze, River was flooded. They were asked to survey the flooding from the air. Landing on flooded fields or lakes, she and Charles carried medicine and food to stranded villagers.

On October 5, they were ready to take off from the river when a wing of their plane was damaged by the churning water. Charles told Anne to pull her life preserver open and jump into the water. Anne jumped, went under, and then came up without choking or feeling any sense of panic. Charles saw her swimming safely, and then he jumped from the plane.

Later, she wrote Elisabeth that she had been careful to drink boiled water the whole time they were traveling—and there she was, "swallowing buckets of Yangtze mud!"

A nearby ship, the British aircraft carrier *Hermes,* rescued them and raised the airplane from the river. Anne and Charles planned to go with the carrier to Shanghai, where the damaged wing would be repaired. But that day, Anne received a telegram from her mother saying that her father had just died. They decided to leave for home immediately, traveling by ship. On board, Anne wrote Con that she couldn't believe their dear father was dead. Though she could not be there for his funeral, his death meant that she could go home to mourn him and to be with Charlie after two long months away.

Anne returned home, hoping that she and baby Charlie would help lift all their spirits if she stayed in Englewood. Charles continued to work for the airlines and was gone for long periods of time. She sent Charlie to Elisabeth's nursery school.

Their Hopewell house was almost finished. Anne wrote her mother-in-law asking her to come visit them. She told story after story of little Charlie. Charles always said, "Hi, Buster" to Charlie, and Charlie mimicked him by responding, "Hi! Hi!" when his father came into the room. But on one December day, when Charles left the room, Charlie said, "Hi all gone."

Anne and Charles moved into their new home in the beginning of 1932. Anne was very happy to be there. She enjoyed being with Charlie and seeing Charles happy with his

work at the Rockefeller Institute. He and Alexis Carrel were doing research on an apparatus that could keep organs alive outside the body. They called it a perfusion machine.

The Hopewell home seemed safe and far from public cu-
riosity, but they only spent weekends there. On Mondays they
left for Englewood so that Charles could be closer to his research in New York, Anne could spend time with her mother,
and Charlie could attend the Little School.

On Monday, February 29, Anne decided she would stay in
Hopewell with Charlie because he had a cold and she was tired
from being up with him during the night. She was also fatigued

*Charles Jr. had his
father's dimpled chin.*

because she was three months pregnant. Charles had stayed in New York City to complete some experiments.

On Tuesday evening, March 1, Charlie was better, and she and Charles decided to leave for Englewood in the morning. Betty Gow had put Charlie to bed. She went upstairs to check on him at eight o'clock and found him sleeping quietly. Charles came home around eight thirty, and he and Anne ate dinner together.

When Betty went back again at ten o'clock, Charlie's crib was empty. She lifted his blankets, felt all around the crib, and found nothing. She ran to Anne's bedroom, thinking she had taken Charlie back to bed with her. When Anne said she didn't have him, Betty raced downstairs to see if Charles had taken the baby with him to his study. Charles said no. He rushed past her up the stairs to the nursery and searched the crib again before shouting, "Anne, they have stolen our baby." He told Oliver Whateley to call the police. Elsie Whateley came upstairs to help Anne and Betty search every room of the house. Within an hour, state police joined local police in their search for baby Charlie.

Anne was in a daze. Later, she asked herself how she could have been "so self-controlled, so calm, so factual, in the midst of horror and suspense?"

Detectives and police, from the FBI and the local and state agencies, soon filled the house, all of them searching for clues. A letter had been found on top of the radiator in the baby's room. No one touched it until the police could dust it for fingerprints. They found none. The kidnappers demanded fifty thousand dollars. The note was filled with misspellings and ended:

> We warn you for making anyding public or for
> notify the Police
> the child is in gut care

Police officials and journalists came to Hopewell frequently after the kidnapping.

Anne spent the first few days after the kidnapping with her mother and sister Elisabeth in her bedroom. The rest of the house was taken over by police officials. She described the confusion: "—a police station downstairs by day—detectives, police, secret service men swarming in and out—mattresses all over the dining room and other rooms at night."

She was certain that the baby would be returned unharmed. Her faith in that belief kept her calm. As day after day went by, she could do little but write reports to her mother-in-law. None of the activity around her made sense.

Anne was told that at Madison Square Garden, a boxing match had been stopped for three minutes while everyone stood to pray for the baby's safe return. They were receiving three to four thousand letters a day, many of them with sympathetic words but some with crazy ideas about how to find the baby. In all the police had counted 12,000 dream letters (the writers saw clues to the kidnapping in their dreams), 11,500 sympathy letters, 9,500 suggestion letters, and 5,000 crank letters.

Charles, trying to remain calm, took charge of the kidnapping investigation. Most of the New Jersey state policemen were young and had little experience in major crime. They were also awed by being with Charles Lindbergh, world hero.

Charles was contacted by a retired teacher, John F. Condon, who had offered to be a go-between with the kidnapper. He would give one thousand dollars of his own money to show that he was serious. An article about him ran in his local newspaper, the *Bronx Home News,* saying, "I stand ready at my own expense to go anywhere, alone, to give the kidnapper the extra money and promise never to utter his name to any person." After the article appeared, Condon received a letter from the kidnapper that told him to place an ad in the *New York American* when he had the money from the Lindberghs.

Charles agreed to let the man exchange the ransom money for the baby. As instructed, Condon met with a man in Woodlawn Cemetery in the Bronx and was told that the group had increased the ransom to seventy thousand dollars and that the baby was fine. To prove it, they would send Condon the sleeping suit Charlie had been wearing.

On Tuesday, March 15, Condon received the baby's sleeping suit, which had been washed and carefully folded. Charles had put together marked money with the help of the Internal Revenue Service. He and Condon drove to the Bergen Greenhouse in the Bronx as they had been instructed. They found a note telling Condon to walk alone into Saint Raymond's Cemetery. Condon left Charles and stood among the headstones in the cemetery waiting for the man they called Cemetery John, who had talked with him in Woodlawn.

Cemetery John told Condon that the baby would not be released for six hours and they should not follow him or start searching for Charlie before then. John gave Condon a note saying that the baby was in good condition and would be found on a boat, the *Nelly,* in the waters near Martha's Vineyard, off Cape Cod, Massachusetts.

Charles waited the six hours, but he had asked President Hoover to have navy planes ready to assist him. He had ordered a plane for himself so he could fly from Connecticut. It was two in the morning by the time he reached Martha's Vineyard. He flew as low as possible, searching for the boat through the night and the next day. He finally gave up. There was no *Nelly* in those waters.

He had to go home and tell Anne the bad news. He had paid the ransom money, but the kidnappers had not returned the baby. To Anne it seemed that time had stopped when the baby was kidnapped. She felt she had been in a "trance state" ever since. In a way, it protected her and the baby she was carrying not to go through all the details Charles was dealing with. Now Charles was breaking through to tell her about his despair.

It had been a month since Charlie was taken. More weeks passed. On April 12, the first marked bill from the ransom money turned up in a Connecticut bakery. Soon other bills were found, but they didn't lead to the kidnappers.

Anne finally began to write in her diary again, after three months of not writing anything except the long letters she sent to her mother-in-law. She warned Charles's mother not to believe all the articles she read in the newspapers. Half of them were inaccurate. Many were completely made up.

On May 12, William Allen was driving along a little-used road near Hopewell. He had stopped and walked into the woods a short distance to stretch his legs when he saw what looked like small human bones in the dirt. He contacted the

local police. They called Colonel Schwarzkopf, head of the
state police, who had befriended the Lindberghs and had
been in charge of the case. Allen took them back to the site,
and Schwarzkopf was almost certain the body was that of the
Lindbergh baby. He removed the clothing on the corpse to
show Betty Gow. She confirmed that the two flannel under-
shirts had belonged to baby Charles. Next, he told Anne's
mother and asked her to go upstairs with him to tell Anne.

Schwarzkopf reported to Anne that he thought the baby's
body had been found in the nearby woods. A skull injury suggested that little Charlie had died immediately after he was
taken. The kidnapper had dropped him as he was climbing

*When Charles Jr.'s body was found in the woods near
Hopewell on May 12, 1932, crowds drove to the site.*

down the ladder outside the window.

Anne wrote in her diary that night that it was a relief to know what had happened. Then her tears would not stop. She relived every moment of her last days with him. How she gave him tender, constant care because of his cold. How she rocked him and sang to him. She wrote long, questioning passages in her diary, wondering how they could have kept Charlie safe.

By the end of May, Anne had another worry. Elisabeth's new medical report was not good. Her heart valve was more damaged than the doctors had thought, and there was no way to treat it. She would probably only live five years more. Elisabeth left on June 1 for Great Britain to spend the summer sitting and reading in the sun.

Anne found she couldn't concentrate on reading or on writing her book about their trip to Asia. She sat with her pad in front of her, but nothing came. She and Charles were staying with her mother because they couldn't tolerate their new home at Hopewell. The property, crowded with reporters and publicity seekers, would always be the house from which Charlie was taken.

Anne and Charles grieved differently. He closed himself off with work, and Anne could do no work at all. But the loss of their son brought them closer.

Letters and telegrams poured in from around the world. They received more than one hundred thousand pieces of mail. Some came from leaders of the country, some from relatives, most from strangers throughout the United States. The Lindbergh baby's kidnapping and death brought worry to parents everywhere. They cautioned their children never to speak to strangers, never to accept candy from them, never to get into a car with a stranger.

SEVEN

After the Kidnapping

*Out of last fall, out of this
winter, a perfect baby. It
was a miracle.*
—Anne Morrow Lindbergh, 1932

After the loss of the baby, Anne tried to find meaning in her life. She continued to write searching entries in her diary. In June, she confessed that she had always taken from her family and friends and decided that it was time for her to stop taking and find ways to give back.

Charlie's birthday, June 22, 1932, was also her birthday. In her diary, she wrote that she thought of him all day, capturing his smiling face in her mind. That night she dreamed of the new baby and heard its laugh, which reminded her of Charlie.

By the end of June, she and Charles moved back to Hopewell. She knew the beautiful, sturdy stone house would always remind her of baby Charlie. It could never be otherwise. But she had to go on. She had to work on her book about their trip, even though she found the writing unsatisfying and the pages not nearly good enough.

Charles decided the only way they could stay at Hopewell and feel safe was to get a dog that would guard the house and all of the people who lived there. He found a German shepherd that had been trained to attack at the command of his trainer. Charles was able to retrain the dog so that it would follow their commands. They called him Thor.

Even with the dog as their security, Anne did not feel safe in the house. The Lindberghs returned to the Morrow home in Englewood, where there were people to help them and guards to protect them. They planned a separate wing in the house for themselves to live in once the new baby was born.

Before the loss of Charlie and her father's early death, Anne had taken for granted that she would have the rest of her life with her friends and with her baby. Now she confided in her diary that she had a constant fear of losing those close to her whenever she said good-bye.

She also wrote about how impatient she was to have the new baby. She was uncomfortable with the pains and heaviness of the pregnancy. Finally, on Monday, August 15, she went into labor during the night. Early the next morning, August 16, 1932, she and Charles drove into New York to meet her doctor and nurse at the Morrow apartment. The streets were empty of people, but there were milk wagons and trucks delivering newspapers and groceries.

Anne's labor lasted about four hours. Her mother and Charles were there with her. The baby was a boy, and he was perfect. Anne was greatly relieved to know that he was all right. "Out of last fall, out of this winter, a perfect baby. It was a miracle," she told her diary. She felt a new surge of life and could see that Charles and her mother were also joyful, although they had both expected a girl. Anne hoped her mother was not disappointed that this baby could not wear the pink, frilly dresses she had brought back from Europe.

Charles told her, "You'll wear the baby out, looking at it." And she did find herself constantly checking him to be sure he was perfect. She thought he looked bigger than Charlie or, at least, longer. He also had the Lindbergh dimple in his chin.

Charles decided they should give the Hopewell house to the state to be used as a children's home. He was sure they would never be able to live in it again, even with the dog and security guards. The bad memories of Charlie's kidnapping would always be part of the house. But he was sure that it could be used for some good purpose. Anne felt it was a way to "make good out of evil." Congress soon passed a bill making kidnapping a federal crime punishable by death. They called it the Lindbergh Law.

By October Charles and Anne finally found the perfect name for their son after reading a Scandinavian history book. They would call him Jon. Jon Morrow Lindbergh. They felt it was a strong name. When Jon was three months old, Anne wrote her mother-in-law that he was now smiling huge smiles whenever she came to get him.

The joy she was feeling in baby Jon was helping her to get past Charlie's death. Anne also was pleased to learn that Elisabeth had met a man in England, Aubrey Morgan, whom she adored. They were married on December 28, 1932, in the Englewood house. Anne thought Elisabeth was *made* to be married and have a happy home."

Dwight was well enough to give his sister away. Con was her bridesmaid; Anne, her matron of honor. Anne said she sensed their father's presence with them that day, blessing each of them. Aunts and uncles, family friends, and

Elisabeth's close friends were crowded together in the library to welcome Aubrey Morgan into the family.

In the summer of 1933, Charles and Anne set out again on a long flight to study transoceanic air routes. Their main goal was to find landing places that were safe and flat for Pan American Airlines planes after they crossed the Atlantic Ocean. This time Anne felt like a full partner, flying when

Empty, Charles and Anne's Lockheed Sirius seaplane weighed 4,600 pounds. But for long trips, such as the northerly route to Great Britain during the Atlantic survey flight of 1933, the plane carried plenty of emergency equipment and supplies on board.

necessary and communicating constantly by radio to stations on the ground. They planned to explore Greenland, Iceland, Denmark, Sweden, Russia, the coast of Africa, and South America. Their plane with pontoons would allow them to land on water wherever it was necessary. Charles expected to be gone about five months.

Again Anne was reluctant to leave the baby, but Charles insisted he needed her. They left on July 9, stopping to say good-bye in North Haven. Jon, almost one year old by then, was staying there with both his grandmothers and his nurse. Anne knew he was surrounded by people who loved him, but that didn't keep her from feeling a lump in her chest—the "going away lump," she called it.

She left Jon a special message in her diary, in case anything should happen to them on the trip. She wrote that she wanted him to grow up a "courageous man—so that he will not be afraid of life but will meet it with optimism and courage and zest like his father and his grandfather."

Once she was in her small cockpit, it became her whole world. She thought of it as her shell, the way a snail has its shell for protection. They flew north, landing in Newfoundland. There they explored two small settlements, Cartwright and Hopedale, where missionaries welcomed them.

Then they flew to Holsteinsborg, a tiny settlement on the west coast of Greenland. In Greenland a special dance was held for them, with two men fiddling and lots of young people dancing English and Irish rounds. Scottish whalers and traders had taught the dances to the Inuit many years earlier. Anne was delighted by the colorful clothing and joyous movements. She compared her pleasure over the country dancing to the pleasure she had from a Bach concert in New York the previous year.

Charles pauses for a photograph with Inuit of Greenland during the Lindberghs' Atlantic survey flight in 1933.

Anne had a pair of boots made for her, dogskin-lined on the bottom and sealskin-lined on top. They were comfortable and kept her warm in the wet, icy weather.

The Inuit children called the Lindbergh's plane *Tingmissartoq,* "the one who flies like a big bird." Anne and Charles decided it was a perfect name for it.

In her diary, Anne described how amazing it was that you "can drop right into the heart of their Inuit life. From being total strangers you suddenly become friends, allies against the outside world." They stayed with one family for less than a week, yet she felt she had formed a "strong bond" with them.

In Copenhagen, Denmark, they stayed at a fancy hotel, and she had to deal with all the "bellboys, carpets, elevators, doormen." She found it just as difficult as always. Anne really preferred staying in the simple homes of the people who treated them like family, rather than in expensive hotels where they quickly became celebrities once again.

On this trip, she often wrote in her diary about finding her own place in the world. "And there is so little time left. I am almost thirty," she wrote. She quoted from a poem by the French poet Paul Verlaine: "And life slips by like a field mouse scarce shaking the grass."

Anne and Charles both loved Stockholm, Sweden. Even when they were recognized, the people there left them alone. Before they left Sweden, they traveled to see the land of Charles's early Swedish relatives. They flew part of the way and then took a motorboat to the village of Gardlosa on the southern coast.

During the Atlantic survey flight, Anne (third from right) and Charles (far right) dined with friends in Copenhagen, Denmark, on August 27, 1933.

"There are fields of cabbages and beets, windmills in the distance, gently rolling fields," Anne wrote in her diary. They met an old man who had known Charles's grandfather. His wife was excited. She kept saying in Swedish that she knew Charles would come back; she had been waiting patiently. She showed Anne the rugs and hangings she and her daughters had woven and gave her a rug to take home. The old man gave Charles some papers he had kept that were written by Charles's grandfather in very beautiful Swedish script, as well as a pair of his grandfather's glasses. They were pleased when Charles signed his name in their family's record book.

From Sweden they flew to Leningrad (present-day Saint Petersburg) and Moscow in Russia. At first Anne was struck

Anne and Charles (center) returned to Russia on their Atlantic survey flight in 1933. Dignitaries welcomed the Lindberghs wherever they landed.

by the poverty and the crumbling of buildings and roads, "crowded streetcars; dull, drab, poor-looking people, but all busy. The feeling of a glittering city gone to decay." She explained to her mother that everything was about the "social point of view," because of the Communist government there. Her guides would not let her forget that she should be aware of the struggle of the people.

Flying southwest, they finally reached Wales, where Elisabeth and Aubrey lived. Her sister had had another heart attack, and Anne found her thin and in constant pain. She and

Anne and Charles (front) also visited the Scottish Shetland Islands on their Atlantic survey trip in 1933.

Aubrey were happy to be together and to see Charles and Anne. The doctors told Elisabeth that the warm weather of California would be better for her health, and they planned to leave Wales soon.

In London, Anne and Charles had dinner with the prime minister of Great Britain, Sir Ramsay MacDonald, at the official residence at 10 Downing Street. He had known Anne's father and showed her the sofa where her father had sat a few years before.

Anne wrote her mother about that meeting and told her that she worked hard not to be shy with new people and as "C. never will stoop to small talk, I have to, and feel I can manage pretty well now."

They spent some time in Killarney, Ireland, where Charles also had ancestors. And then they flew to Paris. Charles was still the hero of Paris, because of his memorable flight in 1927. They tried to see as many people as possible in the city, but Anne was getting tired of talking to people. By the end of November, she could hardly stand it. They had been gone more than five months, and she wanted to be home with Jon and her mother.

After spending time in Spain, they planned to land in Dakar, a city in Senegal, Africa—the closest place in Africa to cross the Atlantic Ocean to South America. Unexpectedly, they received a radio message from Dakar warning them not to come. There was an outbreak of yellow fever there.

They requested permission to land in Bathurst, south of Dakar, in the African country of Gambia. There they spent several days preparing the plane for the long flight across the ocean to South America. Charles knew the plane was too heavy to take off from Bathurst without strong winds, and officials there warned him not to expect them. He removed all the unnecessary weight from the plane, leaving behind an anchor, heavy clothing, boots, ropes, and kerosene.

Early on the morning of December 6, they awoke before four in the morning, took their essential maps and radio instruments, and arranged them in the plane. Once they were both settled into their separate cockpits, Charles released the throttle, and they moved out into the bay. The plane roared along the water. They should have risen into the air, but instead, the noise stopped and the plane sank back into the waves. There was not enough wind to lift them.

Charles began siphoning fuel from the plane to further reduce the weight. They napped that afternoon, in preparation for a night flight. Later, Anne visited lovely gardens near Government House, where they were staying. While sitting outdoors, Anne felt cool air on her face. She held up her handkerchief and watched it flutter in the wind. Strong wind. When she told Charles, he said they would leave at midnight.

There was a full moon that night, reflecting on the bay. The stars in the sky were bright. Again, they settled into their cockpits. Charles released the throttle. The plane surged ahead. Anne was certain they were going to make it this time. And then suddenly the plane sank. It made no sense to her. Charles turned the plane around and tried to take off again, but the wind was gone. The bay was quiet.

He took more weight out of the plane: the oil, the extra gasoline tank, extra food, more tools—almost 150 pounds. He was certain that would help. They would try again the following night. They followed the same routine, resting during the day, coming down to the pier at midnight. Once they were in their cockpits, Charles turned the throttle. The engine was strong. They were moving quickly. More quickly than before. Then the engine lurched and coughed. They were going to crash! "My God—it's coming then—death," Anne thought.

"But it smooths out now, like a long sigh, like a person breathing easily, freely," Anne later remembered. There was wind! Enough to lift them into the air. They moved above the water, sputtering but rising. "We did it, we did it!" Anne cried, recording their departure from Bathurst at 2:00 A.M.

They still had sixteen hours of flying through the night before they reached Natal in Brazil. In her tiny cockpit space, Anne concentrated on transmitting and receiving the dots and dashes of Morse code as they flew the cloudless sky.

They spent a few days in South America, explored Puerto Rico, and were back in the United States by December 16. After five and one half months, they returned to Englewood and found Jon a spoiled but happy boy.

Anne became the first woman to receive the Hubbard Gold Medal from the National Geographic Society for distinction in exploration, research, and discovery. An article in the *New York Times* said, "The boys already have their circumnavigator [of the Earth]. The girls now have theirs."

Awards and articles were not that important to Anne. She was relieved to be back to her own life and to have Jon with her. Charles had decided the safest place for them to live was in a New York apartment, so in the beginning of 1934, they moved from Next Day Hill to East Eighty-Sixth Street. Anne set up a special place in the apartment with her fountain pen, ink, and paper, where she could sit down each day to work on her book about their first trip to Asia. She said she worked "simply by plugging along blindly and stubbornly from day to day." She used her letters to her mother with all their descriptions of people and places. She also reread her diary entries to remind her of her emotional reactions on the trip.

She had to interrupt work on the book to write an article about the recent trip to Greenland for the *National Geographic*. It received excellent reviews, and she was beginning to accept the fact that she was a writer.

Charles and Anne gave the plane *Tingmissartoq* to the American Museum of Natural History in New York. Later, it was moved to the Smithsonian Institution in Washington, D.C.

She and Charles were financially comfortable, as were most of their friends. Many other Americans had lost their jobs and were suffering financially during the Great Depression (1929–1942). Wherever they went on flying trips in the United States, they saw long lines of men trying to get free meals or a chance to work. One day, when their new plane had motor troubles, they landed on a farm in Oklahoma. The neighbors came from all around to meet Anne and Charles and to talk about their farming problems—their crops were poor, there had been no rain, and they barely had enough money to buy seed for the next season.

In the back of a police car, Bruno Hauptmann (right) rides to a Bronx court to face charges for the kidnapping and murder of Charles Jr.

EIGHT

Trial and Loss

How incredible that my baby had any connection with this!
—Anne Morrow Lindbergh, 1935

In September 1934, Anne and Charles flew to Los Angeles to visit Elisabeth and Aubrey, who were enjoying the warmth of California on a friend's ranch. Elisabeth seemed healthier than she had been when they saw her in Wales. The four of them were having a wonderful reunion until Charles received a phone call from Colonel Schwarzkopf of the New Jersey State Police.

Schwarzkopf wanted the Lindberghs to know that the police had a kidnapping suspect, and he hoped they would hurry home. Anne and Charles immediately flew back East. After both of them had reached some peace about Charlie's death, the horror of the kidnapping was starting up all over again.

James Flinn, another New Jersey state police officer, had been charting ransom bills whenever they turned up. At first the bills were found throughout New York City. Later, they were found mainly in Upper Manhattan, in the German-speaking area of Yorkville. Shopkeepers who received them described a customer who fit the description of Cemetery John. Then on September 18, 1934, a gas station attendant received a ten-dollar ransom bill from a man driving a blue Dodge. The attendant wrote down the license number, which turned out to be for a car that belonged to thirty-six-year-old Bruno Hauptmann. At Hauptmann's home, in northeast Bronx, police found more than fourteen thousand dollars of the ransom notes, as well as maps of New Jersey; drawings of a homemade ladder; a small bottle marked "ether," a liquid used to anesthetize people; and paper that matched the ransom notes.

In a lineup at the police station, Charles identified Hauptmann's voice as the voice he had heard from the cemetery. He believed that Charlie's kidnapper had been found. The trial was set for January 2, 1935, in the courthouse in Flemington, New Jersey.

And if that were not enough, in California Elisabeth had emergency surgery for appendicitis. Her mother had rushed to be with her. She was doing well the first few days after surgery, but suddenly she came down with pneumonia and died late on December 3. When the telephone rang in the middle of the night, Anne knew the call was bringing bad news. Anne's mother told them that she and Aubrey would bring Elisabeth's body back to Englewood. They held the funeral in the same room in which Elisabeth and Aubrey had been married two years earlier.

The whole family was shocked and could barely get through the Christmas holiday or prepare for the coming trial. Anne went into a deep depression. She was in tears most of the time and had terrible nightmares about baby Charlie and her sister. This was another unbearable loss for her. She planned to keep Elisabeth's memory close to her by writing poems about her and by talking to friends about her. "I shall never lose her; I have the rest of my life to think about her," she wrote.

When the trial began in January 1935, Charles spent every day in the courtroom. He was glad to have Aubrey with him. Day after day, he appeared at the trial and dealt with everything in a distant, objective way, as though it did not touch him at all.

Charles (center) appeared as a witness on January 3, 1935, at the trial of Bruno Hauptman.

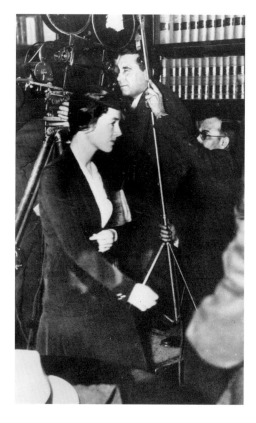

Anne [center] *braces herself to testify at Hauptmann's trial.*

Anne stayed away from the courtroom, except when she was called to the witness stand. She was calm and her voice was strong as she answered the attorney's questions. The onlookers and journalists in the courtroom leaned forward as if they were waiting for her to break down any minute. But Anne did not cry, even when she was handed Charlie's torn clothing or his baby picture to identify. She was able to keep her composure the whole time she was on the witness stand.

Later, she accompanied her mother, Betty, when Betty was called to testify. Then Anne was able to study the scene as she hadn't been able to earlier. She noticed the sad face of

Hauptmann's wife, the faces of the jury, the stenographer taking down the words, the judge sitting quietly. "How incredible that my baby had any connection with this!" she wrote in her diary.

The small town of Flemington overflowed with journalists and photographers, nosy spectators, and vendors selling all sorts of trinkets. The hotel filled up its fifty rooms. Snow had been falling for days. There was a heavy blizzard toward the end of the trial that made it difficult for anyone to reach the courthouse, but still they came.

The papers were filled with daily details of the court proceedings. One columnist described all the "vultures" who were there to watch. It went on week after week, finally ending in early February. The last prosecution witness, Arthur Koehler, had studied the ladder used to kidnap baby Charles from his upstairs bedroom. He could tell where the wood came from and which tools had been used to shape it. He said that a piece of wood in the ladder came from Hauptmann's attic, and that Hauptmann had used a chisel that was later found in the Lindbergh's yard.

The trial ended, and the jury went into deliberation. On the night of February 13, Charles, Anne, and her mother ate dinner with the radio on, just in case a verdict would be announced. At ten forty-five, the announcement came. Bruno Hauptmann was found guilty! He would be put to death in the electric chair.

Charles was convinced this was the right verdict. Many others were not so certain. Hauptmann's wife maintained his innocence to the end of her own life. Anne just wanted it to be over, and she hoped she could put all the grief behind her. She could deal with her emotions only in her diary. Charles wanted her to be strong, to stop crying, and to stop showing

NINE

Living Abroad

*The "simple" life that many
men extol, I learned that
first summer is extremely
complicated for women.*
—Anne Morrow Lindbergh, 1976

For a few years, Charles had been telling Anne that they were not safe in the United States. They often received threatening letters, and they were still besieged by the press whenever they tried to leave Next Day Hill. Charles wanted to settle in Europe where they could live anonymously.

They feared for Jon's safety, even though Thor was an excellent guard dog and they had hired armed guards around the clock. Then one day, the car bringing Jon home from school was forced off the road. A photographer opened the car door and took photos of the frightened child. That did it.

Early in December 1935, Charles decided they were moving to England. Anne had just finished setting up a new apartment away from the house just for writing. The move would interrupt her work on the next book. She was also sorry to be leaving her friends and family. Charles didn't need people in the way she did, to share ideas and books and music. He was quite happy on his own and with her.

Still she began preparing for the move. In a frantic two weeks, she packed everything they would need, including warm coats, sweaters, and blankets for a cold English winter. They left on the evening of December 21, 1935, taking a small ship that would dock in Liverpool, England, ten days later. They were the only passengers, and Jon was happy to find a kitten he could play with on board the ship. Still, he said he was ready to go back to Englewood to be with "Daddy Bee"— his name for Anne's mother.

Arriving in Liverpool, they had to push through the reporters with cameras waiting along the gangplank. In the background, they heard the news sellers calling out, "Lindbergh in Liverpool!"

Anne and Charles, carrying their son Jon, arrive in Liverpool, England, on December 31, 1935.

By then, Anne's father's biographer, Harold Nicolson, was back in England. He offered to rent them his house in Long Barn. He and his wife, Vita, were living nearby in Sissinghurst Castle, and the house in Long Barn was sitting unoccupied. He said he remembered how good the Morrows had been to him when he stayed with them in the United States. He was hoping to return the favor.

The house was in a fourteenth-century village. Nicolson and his wife had planted spectacular gardens there. Nicolson hoped the setting would bring the Lindberghs a peaceful life. Earlier, at Next Day Hill, Nicolson had written to his wife about them: "I like the man. I dare say he has his faults, but I have not yet found them. She is a little angel."

Anne writes at her desk in Long Barn.

The first time Charles and Anne visited the Long Barn house, they stood on the top of the hill and saw the winter gardens and the vast land beyond them. It looked so beautiful they couldn't resist the offer. Inside, they found a two-story house with at least seven bedrooms, all of which opened into one another, since there was no central hall. The original house was built in 1380. The ceilings were sagging, and there were leaks and cracks in the walls too. But all they had to do was look outside to see the gardens, and nothing else mattered.

"This house is terribly higgledy-piggledy," Anne wrote her mother. The lamps didn't plug into the walls, the doors didn't lock, and the pull chains to flush the toilet didn't work, but Anne knew they could find people who would help them put the house in order.

They moved in on March 6, 1936. In the beginning, Anne had trouble believing that they were really living at Long Barn. "For the first week or two . . . I woke up each morning feeling detached and weekendy—like a guest," she wrote to Con. But after she moved the furniture and resettled everything, Anne found a room in which to write and a room for Charles's study. Then she began to feel at home. Working on an early chapter of her second book, she felt that memory was the spiritual part of her life, just as the house was the physical aspect.

On March 7, Germany's new leader, Chancellor Adolf Hitler, sent his troops into an area on the west bank of the Rhine River, called the Rhineland. It was an area that had previously belonged to Germany and had been taken away by the Treaty of Versailles, the peace treaty that ended World War I. Hitler was eager to regain control of that area and rearm it. Anne and Charles were both surprised that Great Britain and the other European countries did nothing to stand up to

Germany's aggressive action. Historians have pointed out that they could have ended Hitler's ambitions that year, if they had acted forcefully against him.

Charles spent a great deal of his time visiting airplane factories in France and Germany for the U.S. government. After his visits, he sent back reports on what he found. In Germany he met Hermann Goring, second-in command under Hitler. Goring took him to see how quickly German factories were building combat planes. He said they could finish five hundred to eight hundred combat planes a month while Great Britain built only seventy and France less than that. Many years later, Charles realized the Germans were exaggerating their production to mislead the United States and Great Britain.

Charles gave a speech at a luncheon in his honor at the Air Club in Berlin. He suggested that aviators had great responsibility to prevent war and destruction. Many people were pleased that he had spoken out about his fears, but some of his friends were concerned that the Germans were using him as a propaganda tool. Jews in Germany were losing their freedoms and being persecuted, yet Charles never spoke out to condemn the anti-Semitism.

At the same time, Hitler had plans to invade Austria. Great Britain and France signed a pact of neutrality instead of confronting the German leader. Charles had warned both Great Britain and France that they needed to build up their military power if they wanted to prevent war with Germany.

Truman Smith, military attaché to the U.S. Embassy in Berlin, tried to arrange a meeting with Adolf Hitler for the Lindberghs, but that did not happen. Instead, Anne and Charles saw Hitler from a distance, when on August 1, 1936, they attended the opening of the Olympic Games being held

Anne [front center] *and Charles* [far right] *visited Nazi officer Hermann Goring* [left] *in his Berlin home in the 1930s.*

in Berlin. They left Berlin the following day, but Charles wrote a friend that Hitler "has done much for the German people," even though he is a "fanatic."

Returning to Long Barn, Anne went back to work on her book about their flight over the Atlantic Ocean from Africa to South America. She decided to call the book *Listen! the Wind,* words she had found in a poem, "Autumn Resignation," by British poet, Humbert Wolfe. She had kept reciting two lines from the poem while they were waiting for enough wind to lift them into the air in Bathurst, Gambia: "Listen! the wind is rising, and the air is wild with leaves."

Although the trip had taken them more than five months to complete, Anne chose to tell only the story of their last ten days, when they had faced great challenges from weather conditions and illness that were not under their control.

She enrolled Jon in a primary school near Long Barn and hired people to run the house and care for the gardens so that she would have time to write. She and Charles walked through the fields at night, enjoying their freedom and safety. Charles was working with scientists at the Pasteur Institute in London. Soon Anne was pregnant again.

They spent a lovely Christmas at Long Barn that year. In the spring, when she was ready to deliver, she and Charles drove to London. She was in labor all the next day, May 12, 1937, which turned out to be Coronation Day for the new king, George VI.

The next morning, Anne gave birth to a third son. They named him Land, Charles's mother's maiden name. As a surprise for Anne, five-year-old Jon came to visit her at the hospital. When she asked him what he thought of the baby, he stood on tiptoes to see him in his crib. "I think very well of him," Jon said. He told her that he hoped his new brother would be a big help to him when they got home. He could pick up "very little sticks" while Jon would continue to gather large logs and branches.

Anne's brother Dwight married in June, and he and his new wife, Margot, came to visit. Dwight had just finished his first year at Harvard Law School, but soon he would display more symptoms of his illness and have to halt his education. Con married Aubrey Morgan, Elisabeth's widower, that June. Anne was pleased that they would be together and knew that neither of them would forget Elisabeth.

On her thirty-first birthday in June, Anne wrote to her mother that Land had given her the most beautiful smile that morning. "A real one that fills his whole face and is, I think, like Daddy's and the blue eyes trying to talk, too. I was so happy—so happy to have on this birthday my two little boys."

Charles told Anne he had work to do in New York, and he wanted her to come with him for Christmas without the boys. This had become the usual pattern they followed when Anne gave birth to a child. Perhaps it was because Charles did not want her to give so much attention to the baby. They left by ship on December 1, 1937, after celebrating an early Christmas with Jon and the baby at Long Barn.

In the United States, Alexis Carrel was continuing work on the pump Charles had designed. Carrel was studying the organs kept alive by the pump and even talked about developing a superior type of man with organs that would never fail.

Jon and Anne enjoyed being outdoors with their dogs at Long Barn.

They stayed in the United States for three months. Anne saw her friends and all the people who visited her mother in Englewood, while Charles worked with Carrel in his New York laboratory.

As the days passed, she missed the boys more and more. It helped that she could be with her mother and Con, Aubrey, and Dwight. When Anne's beloved Grandmother Cutter died in early March 1938, Anne and the others took the train to Cleveland to attend their grandmother's funeral. The following week, she and Charles left on the *Bremen* for Long Barn. Just as they were leaving, the newspapers reported that the Germans had invaded Austria, but Anne and Charles could get no more news while they were on the ship.

She worked on her book during the crossing. At last they were back at Long Barn on Thursday, March 17. "It *is* nice to have you back!" Jon told them, when he climbed onto their bed in the morning. Five-year-old Jon was so happy to see them, he talked and talked without stopping in his very British accent. He told them about the tree stumps he had pushed over and about the "wretched" rat that killed the guinea pigs.

Without asking Anne, Charles was making plans to buy a small French island, called Illiec, near one owned by the Carrels. The island was only four acres with a stone house surrounded by pine trees. Anne did not want to give up the life they had made at Long Barn for the last two years, but the snapshots Charles showed her of the stone house intrigued her.

Anne finally agreed to the move. On June 8, 1938, Charles, Anne, Jon, and Land left for Illiec, the "wild, rocky" island off the coast of Brittany. At first Anne felt as though the Carrels had taken over her life. They advised her about feeding the children, dealing with servants, and everything else.

The stone house had no heat, electricity, or plumbing. While repairs were being made on it, Anne isolated herself as much as she could in order to work on her book. The people she hired to help with children and house did not get along with one another and were uncomfortable living on the island in such primitive conditions. Anne was constantly trying to soothe everyone. She wrote her mother that sometimes she thought it would be easier to do all the work herself. She told her diary that "the 'simple' life that many men extol, I learned that first summer, is extremely complicated for women."

The stone house on the French island of Illiec

Charles spent as much time as possible working and planning future projects with Carrel. Jon loved living on the island. He searched for shells, for "cockles and clams and winkles on the beaches, chas[ed] the chickens out of the kitchen," and worked in the woods helping the men to saw branches and haul them off. When Charles took time from his work, he joined Anne and Jon to search for abalones in their shells along the rocky coast, and then they had fried abalones for lunch.

Somehow Anne found time to keep writing, often at night by lantern, until she finished the manuscript on June 21. It hardly seemed like the book she had started because she had made so many revisions herself and then added Charles's changes and corrections. He drew a picture in black and white for the cover of the book showing stars and the moon with waves along the bottom. She thought it had a strong, modern look.

Alfred Harcourt wrote Anne the moment he finished reading the manuscript to tell her she had done "a grand job." He had a few suggestions for changes she might make, but he told her that reading her words made "publishing worthwhile."

The U.S. government asked Charles to continue studying military airpower—this time in the Soviet Union. Charles wanted Anne to join him. She didn't want to leave, but she wrote in her diary that she had to go with Charles whether she wanted to or not. She could not give in to her fear or her strong desire to stay home with the children. On August 17, 1938, they flew to Moscow, where Russian citizens turned out en masse to watch the Lindberghs' plane land in the glare of bright searchlights.

Anne had an opportunity to meet Russian women who were well-respected aviators, but she saw that most Russian women worked hard and had little prestige or financial security. Charles visited airplane factories, and he was a guest at many air shows. He didn't feel the quality of Russian planes was equal to those of

In 1938 Charles (left) and Anne flew to Moscow in a Miles Mohawk airplane.

Germany or Great Britain, but he thought they would be adequate for combat.

Anne and Charles flew to Munich, Germany, on October 18. Charles was scheduled to attend a dinner given by Ambassador Hugh Wilson at the U.S. Embassy. The ambassador hoped to talk with Goring about easing restrictions on Jews, who were forced to leave Germany "in a penniless condition," unable to take money or possessions with them.

During the dinner, Goring unexpectedly presented Charles with a small red box. Charles was startled. When he opened the box, he found the German Cross. The German government had presented the military medal to Charles "for his services to the aviation of the world and particularly for his historic 1927 solo flight across the Atlantic." Charles accepted the medal and thanked Goring for presenting it.

For years afterward, Anne insisted his acceptance did not mean that he approved of Hitler's regime or that he had done anything for them. But she knew how the world would view the medal and knew that it would be an enormous problem for them. She told Charles that the medal would be "an albatross"—a terrible burden—around their necks.

Within a few weeks, on November 9, 1938, members of Hitler's Nazi Party attacked Jews, their shops, and their synagogues in Berlin and in other cities throughout Germany. Jews were rounded up and sent to concentration camps. The night of attacks was called *Kristallnacht,* "the Night of Broken

Rioting Nazi Party members broke into Jewish-owned shops in Berlin, Germany, on the evening of November 9, 1938. The event came to be known as the Night of Broken Glass.

Glass." Hitler excused the attacks by saying they came in response to the assassination of the German consul in Paris by a young Jewish man whose parents had been deported.

On Illiec, Anne and Charles read about the attacks in the newspapers. "You just get to feeling you can understand and work with these people [the Germans] when they do something stupid and brutal and undisciplined like that. I am shocked and very upset," Anne wrote in her diary.

Charles had been making plans for them to live in Berlin. He immediately canceled those plans, but that didn't stop the world newspapers from calling Charles "a lackey and henchman of the Nazi Reich," or "a German spy." Most of them insisted that he return the "Nazi medal."

Anne's mother and Aubrey came to visit in early November. Her mother brought Anne mail that had been sent to Englewood, as well as positive reviews of *Listen! the Wind.* These came as a pleasant surprise after all the other negatives in their lives. Anne's book was selling well and received the American Booksellers Association Award for favorite nonfiction in 1939.

In early December, Anne and Charles packed up what they would take from Illiec. They planned to spend the winter in Paris, where the weather would be milder than on the island. In October and November, the sea had become wilder and the storms beat down on them.

Anne left with the children on Saturday, December 3, 1938. They had packed up the cart with all their belongings, and in the early evening, she and the children climbed on top of everything. The tide was low enough to allow them to cross the wet rocks and mud. The cart would take them to their car, and then they would drive to the train. They traveled by night train to Paris and their new apartment near the Bois de Boulogne, a very large park.

Once they were settled, Anne took six-year-old Jon to the park. He was not impressed. He told her that it was too crowded with people. Anne found a wilder area, where there were dead trees and seed pods all over the ground. By the time they returned to the apartment, Jon thought the Bois was the best place in Paris. He said it reminded him of Illiec. Jon started school and seemed happy, though he told Anne he didn't quite understand what the teacher was saying because she spoke only in French.

All the news their family and friends sent from home disturbed them. One letter said that there were bad feelings against Charles for his trips to Germany and the fact that he had thought to live there. In her diary, Anne wrote that "this is just the beginning of a long period of struggle and hate." She wondered how they would get through it.

She wrote her mother that she kept hearing about the "campaign" against Charles in the States. "C. is not and never has been anti-Semitic . . . . The ball of rumor and criticism, once it starts rolling, is difficult to stop." The Lindbergh name was taken off a line of airplanes. Anne worried that Jewish booksellers were boycotting her books.

Despite the ominous political concerns in their lives, Anne tried to find enjoyable activities for the children in Paris. One January morning, she and Jon walked down busy Avenue Victor Hugo. She bought Jon a hydrogen balloon from the balloon man. That afternoon they climbed the Eiffel Tower, and from the high platform, Jon studied the trains going over the bridges below. He told her he counted sixteen of them. When she put him to bed in the evening, they talked about all they had done that day. Jon thought it had been a perfect day. "Sixteen trains and a balloon!" he crowed joyfully.

The newspapers wrote that Charles had sent reports about German aviation to the U.S. government and that he urged a buildup of airplanes in the United States to match Germany's numbers. In her diary, Anne wrote that Charles was considered both pro-Nazi and anti-Nazi. She expressed concern about what would happen to the world. In her college years, she had read Erich Maria Remarque's book, *All Quiet on the Western Front,* a disturbingly frank novel about World War I, and it had turned her against war. She thought of herself as a pacifist, a person who is opposed to war.

In March 1939, Samuel Sloane, her new Harcourt Brace editor, came to dinner at their Paris apartment. He told her that "they consider her an important author!" and she thought it was "terribly funny," but she was grateful for his careful editing and support when she worked with him.

Charles sat for a bronze model of his head sculpted by Jo Davidson, an American sculptor living in France. Davidson was a large, jolly man who completed the head in less than a month. Charles wanted to have one made of Anne and chose Charles Despiau, the French sculptor, who was known for creating more delicate work. He was just the opposite of Davidson—a thin, neurotic man who seemed to be powerless until he started working with the clay. Then he came to life.

For her first sitting, Despiau placed Anne on a tall stool in front of him. He had two lumps of gray clay and began to build up the clay on an armature, or support. He told her that "the likeness, the expression is the last thing to come—you must let it come by itself and be patient." Anne realized that this was true for life and for writing. And for sculpting.

It took him months to complete the head. She could sympathize with his slow, careful work because it was exactly the way she worked. She was quite pleased with the bronze bust he created. While it didn't look exactly like her, she felt Despiau had captured her essence. She wrote in her diary that his head has that "extra thrill of surprise . . . the mystery that is in every human being."

In the background of their lives, war talk was everywhere, in headlines, on the radio, in discussions with their new acquaintances, and in letters from home. Visiting London in 1938, Anne saw lines of people waiting to buy gas masks to protect them during the expected bombings. Meanwhile, Germany had sent troops into Prague, Czechoslovakia, in the modern-day Czech Republic, and planned to move through Romania. There were rumors that Lithuania, Estonia, Latvia, Poland, and Denmark were given ultimatums that they would be next.

Anne and Charles decided it was time to return to the United States. He left by ship on April 8. He was to contact General Henry "Hap" Arnold, chief of the air corps, as soon as he returned. Charles hoped to "take whatever part [he] could in preventing a war in Europe."

On April 20, 1939, Anne and the children left from Le Havre, France, on the ship, *Champlain.* Anne wrote in her diary, "I see France and England, and everything over here I love, going under."

TEN

Coming Home

*My mind has been quickened,
and my sight and feelings.*
—Anne Morrow Lindbergh, 1939

Anne was happy to be back safely in the United States with her family, but she had been out of the country for two and a half years. It would take time for her to adjust. Con, Dwight, and their spouses and babies were all staying at the Morrows' Englewood home. It was a crowded, busy household, and Anne longed to find a place where she and the boys could be alone. Charles was flying all over the country inspecting airplane factories and military installations.

The press seemed to welcome them. *Life* magazine put a picture of Anne on the cover with a caption describing the success of her books. No longer was Charles the only celebrity in the family.

She and Charles found a house to rent at Lloyd Neck, Long Island, with a nearby airfield for his convenience and a lovely setting for all of them. They moved in on Anne's thirty-third birthday, in June 1939. She had decided that she would devote her life to her writing and that this wonderful house, close to the sea, would inspire her.

In August Anne met the French aviator and writer, Antoine de Saint-Exupéry, who had written the preface to the French version of her second book, *Listen! the Wind.* He had written an exquisite book about flight and spirituality called *Wind, Sand and Stars.* Anne had driven in to pick him up at his hotel in New York City. When she first saw him, she was taken aback by his appearance. He was bald and stooped, not at all handsome. She had expected him to be as handsome as his words were. His preface to her book showed that he had read it with great understanding and had discovered beneath the words the sensitive woman who had written them.

As they drove away from the hotel, Anne's car stalled. They had to get the car to a garage and find a taxi to Penn Station, where they would take a train back to Lloyd Neck. The whole time they spoke in French or broken English and found they shared so much about writing, about flying, about life.

Antoine de Saint-Exupéry

Then they discovered they both loved the work of the German poet, Rainer Maria Rilke. Once they were home, they continued talking for hours until Charles arrived home around ten o'clock. Then Anne let the two of them speak about flying and wherever it led them, translating as they needed her. Anne confided in her diary, using Rilke's words: "I feel as though I had been sleeping for years" and had now come fully awake.

Saint-Ex, as they called him, stayed at Lloyd Neck for the next two nights, which gave Anne and Charles a chance to talk continuously with him about the world situation and their shared fascination with flying. Anne also found time to discuss with him the creation of poetry that combines the familiar with the strange—or combines two ideas that seem opposites. Anne translated all of their conversations. She said her "mind was stretched" as far as it could go as she found the proper French words to use. She felt as if she had met "a person who has the same thought" as her own, and she wanted to "cry out for joy."

Anne and Saint-Ex never saw each other again. Still, she felt he had understood her books in a deeper way than anyone else she knew and had validated her writing. In her diary, she wrote about "this absolute stranger who understood so well everything I said and felt!" It was the "first time anyone had talked to me purely on my *craft* . . . not because I was my father's daughter or C's wife."

After Saint-Ex left, she was eager to work, to express the beauty of the world. "My mind has been quickened, and my sight and feelings," she explained. One day, while she was working in her garage office, she heard Jon outside. He had climbed to the top of a tree and was singing and yodeling happily. She had to stop and run out to share his joy.

Later, while she was working at her desk, Charles brought her a folder full of his correspondence that needed to be answered. If she took on this responsibility, she knew she would never get to her own work. She was reviewing Saint-Ex's book for the *Saturday Review,* and it had a strict deadline. She found it difficult to say no to Charles, but this time she did.

The news from Europe was bad. Germany continued to threaten nearby countries. On August 19, 1939, Germany seized Czechoslovakia (the present-day Czech Republic and Slovakia). By August 28, news commentators said that war was coming. The chances were 80–20 for war, they said. It sickened Anne to hear such discussions, as though the on-coming war were a horse race or ball game.

On September 1, 1939, Hitler's army invaded Poland. Great Britain immediately declared war against Germany, as it had said it would. Anne was afraid of what that meant for them and for all their friends in Europe.

In the middle of her emotional turmoil, she received a warm letter from the *Saturday Review,* saying that her review of *Wind, Sand and Stars* was excellent. They didn't plan to make a single change. Anne was pleased, but the war news made her review seem unimportant—"an incredible lightness and joy that does not belong to this period."

Anne and Charles listened to President Franklin Roosevelt on the radio on September 4. He assured the country that the United States would not enter the European conflict. On Friday, September 15, Charles gave a radio speech while he was in Washington, D.C., saying that he also hoped the United States would stay out of the war. His speech was featured in the newspapers the next day and telegrams poured in, most of them agreeing with Charles's thoughts.

On September 15, 1939, Charles gave a speech encouraging the United States to stay out of World War II (1939–1945).

Many British newspapers were not happy with his speech, especially since he had lived and found safety in that country. The French also were upset with his ideas.

Anne couldn't write for weeks. The war news had taken over her life. Charles was getting hate mail from people who called him a Nazi for not wanting the United States to enter the war. One correspondent said he was pro-Nazi because he had accepted that German medal. There were letters threatening their children.

By the end of November, Anne finished "Prayer for Peace," an article that was published in the *Reader's Digest,* in January 1940. She began the article admitting that she was not an expert on the history of war. But she saw that the original agreements after World War I were unfair in the way they divided up Germany. This left the German people feeling great resentment. She also pointed out that if the United States had supported the League of Nations, this would have given security to all European countries. She was only twenty when she had attended early sessions of the League in Europe, but she remembered the hope everyone had felt for what the League could accomplish.

Still, she was aware that the experiences of the past did not excuse Germany's aggression toward its neighbors. She wrote in her article that she prayed going to war could still be prevented and that the United States would lead in calling for a peaceful solution. When readers chose it as their favorite article in the *Reader's Digest,* Anne was pleased to know that the Lindbergh name still could be received in a positive way.

In the spring of 1940, Anne discovered that she was again pregnant. She was very happy about having another child, even though the world situation was not a happy one. The newspapers and radio announced on April 16 that Germany had invaded Denmark and Norway. Anne couldn't bear to

Nazi forces began to invade Norway on April 9, 1940.

think of those countries overtaken by troops and tanks, especially when her life was good and she was surrounded by the beauty of early spring bulbs, trees leafing out, and the new life she was carrying.

Charles took the whole family flying one afternoon. It was the first time three-year-old Land understood that he was in the air. At first he was wary, but then he looked down to see tiny automobiles, and he forgot his concerns. Seven-year-old Jon shared Anne's ecstasy in the air. Her sons were finding the freedom of the sky that she had always valued.

In May the Germans invaded Holland and Belgium and were moving toward France. This made the war even more personal for Anne. She loved France, and she had many friends there. At the end of May, she read in the newspaper that Saint-Exupéry was safe, although he had faced many close calls. She feared for his life as well as the lives of many "beautiful young men, doomed to be downed by fate, just fate."

Daily she worried that she was not writing, because she was consumed by war news. She remembered what the sculptor Despiau told her: "If you have three moments of clear vision in a day it is enough!" But she wondered what he recommended for the remaining hours.

Ideas began to take shape in her mind, and she decided to write an article expressing her thoughts about the war and explaining her support for Charles's ideas. Harcourt published her essay as a small book, *The Wave of the Future.* In a letter to her mother, she wrote that the article "attempts to give a *moral* argument for Isolationism." She extended many of the ideas in the "Prayer for Peace" article she had written for *Reader's Digest.*

The book became a best seller almost overnight, read and reviewed by many who agreed with Lindbergh's pacifist philosophy. But it also became the "book people loved to hate," and it was misquoted constantly by both sides. Harold L. Ickes, secretary of the Interior, called Charles a Nazi and said that Anne's book was the "Bible of every American Nazi."

Both Anne and Charles opposed the United States going to war against Germany. Anne's mother urged the United States to aid Britain, France, and the Netherlands. They need our help, she pleaded, even if Germany turns against us.

The papers made a great fuss over the fact that Betty Morrow disagreed with her son-in-law and her daughter. In December Betty was bold in her response to newspaperman William Allen White: "Colonel Lindbergh and I differ about what our country's attitude towards the war should be, but each honors the sincerity of the other's opinions and there is no misunderstanding between us."

In the midst of this public controversy, Anne and Charles's first daughter, Anne Spencer, was born on October 2, 1940. Later, they decided to call her Ansy to avoid confusion between mother and daughter. Her birth allowed Anne to stay out of the public eye for a while.

Charles joined a group called America First, whose members came from all kinds of religious and political groups. Members included Gerald Ford, who was elected to Congress after the war; writer and activist Alice Roosevelt Longworth (daughter of former president Theodore Roosevelt); and writer Kathleen Norris. Their main objective was to keep the United States out of the European war. Charles was one of their favorite speakers, and he drew huge crowds whenever he spoke.

On September 11, 1941, in Des Moines, Iowa, Charles gave an extremely controversial speech for America First. In

Ansy joins her big brothers Jon and Land at play outdoors in 1941.

the speech, Charles blamed three groups for "pressing this country toward war." They were the Roosevelt administration, the British, and the Jews.

"It is not difficult to understand why Jewish people desire the overthrow of Nazi Germany," he continued. "The persecution they suffered in Germany would be sufficient to make bitter enemies of any race. No person with a sense of the dignity of mankind can condone the persecution of the Jewish race in Germany." Yet he still did not think that taking the United States into the war was the answer to preventing Jewish persecution.

Jewish people who heard his speech over the radio remember they heard their great hero, Charles Lindbergh, blaming them for promoting war because they were Jewish, rather than seeing them as victims of German fanaticism.

Years later, Anne was interviewed on *60 Minutes* by jour-
nalist Morley Safer. Anne, then seventy-three, said that she
had "tried to prevent [Charles] from delivering [that speech]
and had failed." She knew that people would call him an anti-
Semite even though he wasn't one. She also knew that his
words would be misunderstood and would bring them even
more hate mail than they already received. She justified his
thinking by saying that Charles "was not a great reader." If he
had read Hitler or Goring, he would have known that his
words sounded just like their words. And they were real anti-
Semites.

Columnists, government leaders, Jewish groups,
Catholics groups—all rose up against Lindbergh. One columnist stated that the "Lone Eagle had plummeted from 'Public
Hero No. 1' to 'Public Enemy No. 1.'" His friend Harry
Guggenheim insisted Charles was not anti-Semitic, and others sent their support to him in letters. But there were many
more angry letters from all around the country. Charles saved
every letter, regardless of what it said about him.

When the Japanese attacked Pearl Harbor, Hawaii, on December 7, 1941, Charles found no room for any further dis-
sent. He at last agreed that the United States had to respond
to the attack and join the war. President Roosevelt quickly declared war against Japan. The following week—Thursday, December 11—when Germany and Italy declared war on the
United States, Congress declared war on both Germany and
Italy. Charles hoped to enlist in the air force, but because of
his previous isolationist beliefs, none of the military leaders
were willing to accept his offer.

Anne wondered how she could help the war effort. Con
was organizing women in a Fight for Freedom campaign. So
was her mother. But Anne was pregnant again, and she knew

On December 7, 1941, Japanese bombs poured down on Pearl Harbor, Hawaii. Twenty-one ships sank or were destroyed, and more than 2,400 Americans died. The attack shattered the United States's isolation from the war.

the pregnancy would keep her restricted and ill for months, just as the previous ones had. As she felt better, she enjoyed her beautiful surroundings of water and sky. She also listened to music, especially that of her favorite composer, Johann Sebastian Bach. She read Saint-Exupéry's new book, *Flight to Arras,* which was published in installments in the *Atlantic* magazine.

Anne felt a deep closeness to Saint-Ex's words as he described the "anguish of our age." When she bought a copy of the book, she saw that his earlier book was listed on the jacket but that her preface and her praise had been removed from it. It meant that her name had become just as negative as Charles's. She too had become a pariah, an outcast.

Bundled up against the chilly air, Anne seems to have a lot on her mind in this photograph taken in the early 1940s.

ELEVEN

Serious Writer

*He spoke "my language"
better than anyone I have
met, before or since.*
—Anne Morrow Lindbergh, 1944

The family moved into Seven Gates Farm on Martha's Vineyard off Cape Cod, Massachusetts, for the winter. There were climbing roses and three pine trees standing in front of the house. Below the house was the comforting sea. It was a dark, old-fashioned place, but at least it had heat and was not so close to New York City. Anne knew she could make it feel comfortable.

While they were getting settled, Anne had watched Charles writing his book about the 1927 solo flight to France. He sat at his desk in the middle of the bare living room while the movers worked all around him. He never stopped. "I watch him, enviously remembering that fever of absorption

119

with which one works when one has struck a vein of gold," she wrote in her diary.

After weeks of working to settle into the house, she wrote in her diary, "I want to stop being a good housekeeper. . . . I want to go back again to being a bad housekeeper and a good writer!" Since the house was small, Charles had a room-size tent set up outside for both of them to use as an office.

Anne could not work without interruption. If Charles needed her, if the children wanted her, she had to stop writing, no matter how inspired she felt. It didn't matter that she had household help. The help couldn't substitute for her. She questioned this difference between her and Charles in her diary: "Can one be a good mother and write? Can one be a writer for half the day? I oscillate between the two."

By March 1942, Charles had found a job with Henry Ford's aviation factory in Detroit, Michigan. At first he came home on weekends, but Anne needed more. Once he started

Land, Jon, Anne, and Ansy explore the outdoors in 1942.

answering her letters, though, she was relieved. She realized that they were not separated spiritually, only physically, and she could deal with all the decisions of being alone once she knew that.

Their correspondence during this separation became very meaningful. It was a way for them to say things to each other that they might not have been able to share in person. After a long weekend, when Anne and Jon had visited Charles in Detroit, he wrote to her on April 28, that her essence was "something far above and far beyond . . . you have a touch of divinity in your pen. It is what I have felt ever since I have known you. I feel it more strongly with every year that passes."

Anne was quite moved by his letter. She called it a love letter and said that one does not say "thank you" for a love letter. One thinks only, "Why should I ever ask for anything else if I have this?"

Soon Charles and Anne decided they had had enough separation, and Charles rented a house for the family in Bloomfield Hills, a wealthy community outside Detroit. In early July 1942, they moved in. The house was showy and more formal than Anne liked. She wondered how she could manage to make this place comfortable. She put a lot of things away and kept thinking, "If only it were bare—not all this false elegance!"

Charles brought home a trailer and drove it into the woods at the back of the house. It would be Anne's place to work. She felt more at peace in the trailer than in the house.

The children came by train with their nurse at the end of July. Jon, almost ten, was to go to overnight camp soon. Land was five. Ansy would be two in a few months. They were not overwhelmed by the house. Land did somersaults on the carpets and drummed on the piano keys, while little Anne followed him around. Jon found places to enjoy in the woods near his mother's trailer.

On August 13, 1942, Scott was born. Anne continued reading the papers describing all the horrors that were happening in France and Holland, and the "planned extermination of all Jews in Europe by the Nazis. In moments like these I feel I cannot bear it." She looked at her baby and wondered how "such terrible things exist in the same world?"

Whenever she found a free hour or two, Anne went out to the trailer to work. She was writing a novel about a couple flying over the Alps who have problems with the plane and are about to crash. The wife is pregnant, and Anne remembered what it was like to be cramped in a tiny cockpit while well along in a pregnancy. She remembered the times they had experienced close calls. She gave her character many of the thoughts she'd had, including the possibility that she would lose the life of her child as well as her own if they crashed.

Often she had to break away from her fictional world to deal with her very real children. As he was growing up, Jon had moments of gloom very much like her own. She tried to comfort him and teach him how to get past the difficult times. Jon and Land squabbled a lot, and she had to find ways to separate them. Land loved to play act. Jon liked real work. Anne put him to work shoveling the snow.

Once her book was finished, Charles thought she should wait to publish it. He felt the public was not ready to accept a book from either of them. Anne didn't agree. She knew she wouldn't be able to work on anything new if she put the finished manuscript into a drawer, so she sent it to her publisher.

After he read the manuscript, Alfred Harcourt assured her that it should be published. "[I]t is about a flight of the spirit as well as about the flight of a plane.... The last two or three chapters are, I'd guess the best writing you have done so far," he told her.

Charles had completed his work at Ford and was ready to take a job working for United Airlines, testing their planes. Anne admired the way he had handled his rejection by the government after he volunteered for duty. Rather

Anne with her children (from left). Ansy, baby Scott, Jon, and Land, gather for an outdoor photo in 1943.

than being resentful, he found another way to work. He had studied whole new aspects of his field—high-altitude flying and assessing fighter performance. He had just returned from San Diego and found the night flying beautiful. "When I see something very beautiful, then I think of you," he told Anne.

Anne read Saint-Ex's new book, *The Little Prince.* It was written for children, yet Anne felt it was "not for children *at all.* . . . His Little Prince is a saint, not a child," she wrote in her diary. Anne felt that the sadness in the story was a reflection of Saint-Ex's eternal sadness about the world at war. A few days later, she read in the newspaper that Saint-Ex had joined the French air corps and left for active duty.

She shared *The Little Prince* with Jon, who loved nature and was always planting or caring for the shrubs and trees around their houses. He was distraught that one of the bean plants he was tending looked as though it were dying. He had watered it every day and turned it toward the sun, but its leaves still looked yellow. Anne knew what a sensitive child Jon was. She tried to explain that there would be "failures with any living things because life is uncertain. . . . You can't control it completely." A few days later, his bean was still alive. She reminded him of what the fox told the Little Prince: "It is the time you have devoted to your rose that makes your rose so important."

Charles often took the children to spend Sundays with his mother in nearby Detroit. They called her *Farmor,* the Swedish name for "grandmother." Anne tried to work on her writing in the trailer while they were away. She brought her diary up to date, but as always she heard Charles's voice in her head saying, "Don't waste time on your diary." Still she had to. She knew that working on her diary was a "warming-up process for writing."

Anne turned thirty-seven in the summer of 1943. That summer Jon went to a camp in Wyoming. He was eleven. Six-year-old Land went to a camp close to home. The house was suddenly quiet without Land banging on the piano or throwing all the living room pillows on the floor. Anne missed the children but found she had time to begin a sculpting class at the nearby Cranbrook Academy of Art. She did line drawings from live models to help her understand the body, and she learned how to build a three-dimensional clay figure.

She and three-year-old Ansy spent two weeks that summer in Maine. Being alone with her daughter made her remember all the previous summers she had spent there with her sisters. She treasured getting to know her small daughter better and seeing Maine through her young eyes.

In September the family moved again to another rented house in Bloomfield Hills. By then Anne had lost track of how many houses they had lived in. She, again, worked to get this house organized and comfortable. And she constantly wondered who she was: the "[self] I was last summer at art school, and the one I was in Maine, Anne's mother, and C.'s wife, and the writer I am to Harcourt and Brace. [Or] the real me I am with friends, and this house-tidier. The image is blurred. It is like an astigmatism of the soul." (An astigmatism is an eye problem that causes objects to look distorted.)

She made the small changes Alfred Harcourt had suggested on the manuscript for her novel, *The Steep Ascent,* and sent it back to the publishers. At the same time, she felt how inappropriate a flying story was for the present day, when sixty planes had been lost in a raid on Germany and six hundred men were dead.

Life in the family was busy and distracting. She wrote in her diary, "Frogs in the bathtub, snakes in the bedroom, caterpillars on the windowsill, walnuts on the rug! Chestnuts *everywhere*—what it is to have boys!"

During this time, Charles was often away, testing airplanes. When he was gone, Anne felt a terrible loneliness and pressured herself to find a new subject for a book and to keep writing in her diary. It helped that she was still taking the sculpture class and that she had started a clay head that she was pleased with.

On Christmas Eve, the whole family came together. Jon had made a stand for the tree. Land found the perfect star and brought some grass for baby Jesus's cradle in the Nativity scene. They lit candles and sat in front of the fire, listening to carols on the phonograph. Anne read verses from the Bible. It was a quiet moment for all of them—one of the nicest ever.

In the new year, Anne went back to the Cranbrook studio to work on another sculpture. She had discovered Despiau's "moment of beauty" and felt her recent sculpture showed that beauty. It was a process similar to writing, when she went deep into her unconscious to find those hidden thoughts.

Every evening that spring of 1944, she edited the chapters for Charles's book as he revised them. He was finishing *The Spirit of St. Louis,* his title for his book on his 1927 solo flight to Paris.

Her novel, *The Steep Ascent,* came out that March. Anne could hardly wait to read the reviews. Most of them were stinging criticisms of her book as an "unimportant finger exercise" or "egotistical escapism." The one that hurt most said, "Because Saint-Exupéry was relatively unknown in this country her writing seemed good." It was crushing to think that her work would be compared so unfavorably to Saint-Ex. Later reviews were better and sales were good, but nothing could remove the sting of those early negative reviews.

Charles came home one day and told Anne that he was going to the South Pacific to bring his expertise to the airplanes he had tested. He left in early April as excited as a boy going off on a new adventure. He soon wrote her that the servicemen he met accepted him completely and respected his careful rating of planes and the fuel consumption techniques he had developed.

Anne continued her sculpting classes at Cranbrook. Teachers and students became her friends and gave her the intellectual stimulation and companionship she needed. She missed Charles while he was away, but she handled life on her own with the four children. She dealt with the daily complications caused by the war, such as rationing of butter, meat, sugar, and rubber, as well as gasoline for the car.

Charles (second from left) visited fighter pilots on Emirau Island in the South Pacific in May and June 1944.

Suddenly, on August 9, Anne's life was disrupted by a terrible shock. She had read in the newspaper that Saint-Exupéry was missing over southern France after a solo reconnaissance flight. Anne could hardly accept the news. It reminded her of the shock she had when baby Charles was found dead or when Elisabeth died suddenly. "The heart will not take it all at once; it rejects it, it has to be told—a fresh telling . . . over and over again," she wrote. For months she hoped he would be found.

His loss made her question the value of her writing: "Of what use to write if he were not there to read it?" She was certain he was the one person in the world who understood her words. Theirs was only a single contact, yet she felt "he spoke 'my language' better than anyone I have ever met, before or since."

At the end of August, Charles cabled that he was in Australia and on his way home. Anne had made a trip to Connecticut and found the perfect house for them near the United Aircraft factory, where Charles would be working when he returned.

The rented house was in Westport, a community with good schools. It had trees and a brook surrounding it. Also, it was unfurnished, which meant Anne at last could move in their own belongings. She wanted to stop living with other people's taste, and she wanted to be with Charles and not have him constantly commuting long distances to work.

By that fall, Charles had returned, the children were in school, and she had set up her desk in a small alcove next to the bedroom. She had not written steadily in her diary since July, but seeing her pen, ink, blotter, and paper waiting for her was a good sign that life was settling down. She told her diary that she could not "start life over again" until she had examined those past months. "I must let my soul catch up" with me, she wrote. She found time to walk through the trees and to throw crumbs for the birds, as she had done everywhere they lived.

The war in Europe ended in May 1945, after nearly six long years of battle, hardship, and death. Hitler's Germany was defeated by the Allies—the British, American, French, and Russian troops. Hitler killed himself in his German hideout before the soldiers could capture him. His regime had killed millions of Jews and other innocent people.

It would take many years before European countries could rebuild their cities and return to normal life. Anne had kept in touch with their friends in Europe and knew of their struggles. In the United States, she and Charles were spared such difficulties. They had built a large stone house for their family in Darien, Connecticut, which Anne figured was their tenth move in fifteen years.

She was thirty-nine and pregnant with her sixth child. Those early months were just as difficult as always. Their daughter Reeve was born on October 2, 1945, exactly five years after her sister Anne's birthday on October 2, 1940.

The children led busy lives, and Anne was responsible for getting them to lessons, to sports, to doctors and dentists, in addition to supervising everything at home. Charles was often away as an air force consultant. And when he was gone, the atmosphere in the house changed. Everyone relaxed, knowing that their father would not pull out his long list of chores or scold them for a small misdemeanor. "[W]e could feel a delicious looseness leaking into our very bones," daughter Reeve later wrote in her memoir. When Charles came home, he pulled out his lists, and supervised their lives.

In those busy years after the war, *Reader's Digest* magazine asked Anne to travel to Europe to find out how various

The thought of leaving baby Reeve (left) *and her older siblings made it difficult for Anne to agree to take a three-month writing assignment in Europe.*

countries were dealing with postwar life. At first she said she couldn't possibly go. She couldn't leave the children. Jon was thirteen, Land, eight, Anne, five, Scott, three, and there was the baby Reeve. Charles urged her to go. He said he and the staff could take care of everything.

Anne was away two months and then worked daily in another trailer parked near their home, where she wrote five different articles for *Reader's Digest, Life,* and *Harper's* about the sad conditions she had found in France, Germany, and Great Britain. She wrote: "All of Europe reduces itself to one bleak stark picture. Europe is hungry—for food, for material, for hope."

She also described how shockingly different commercial flying was from her personal experience of flying in a small plane with Charles. She described having to deal with terminals, crowds of people, and being shuffled into a tight, cramped space without any joyful sense of being in the air. She had never complained about that tight, cramped cockpit when she flew with Charles, because she had been his partner and her skills had been crucial to the success of the flight. Modern "flying has shut out the sky," she complained.

TWELVE

Gift from the Sea

*What a circus act we women
perform every day of
our lives.*
—Anne Morrow Lindbergh, 1956

In 1948 Anne, Charles, and the children went to Captiva Island in southwestern Florida, where she and Charles had spent vacations alone in earlier years. Anne found it a perfect place, with the Gulf of Mexico on one side of the narrow island and the bay on the other. She couldn't wait to return.

Two years later, Anne left the children at home and went back to the island alone. She stayed in a cottage right on the beach. In the mornings, she tried to write after she did the least amount of housekeeping necessary. Usually that meant sweeping the gritty sand out the front door and returning it to the beach. In the afternoons, she walked along the beach, looking for herons or gulls to feed, finding shells as the waves flowed in and out. She kept her meals as simple as possible

132

and relished the solitude. She found the peace and quiet allowed her to delve deep into her own thoughts. Anne studied the shells she found on the beach, equating them with the stages of her life—of any woman's life—and decided to write a book about what she was learning.

For each chapter, she chose a shell. The channelled whelk stood for a simple life, perhaps the romantic beginning of a marriage. The moon shell was a milky-white circle reminding her to keep time for herself in the center of her growing family. The double-sunrise shell told her to keep time for her husband within the busy family. The oyster shell represented the middle years of marriage, with its "heavily encrusted" growth, so similar to the many responsibilities parents face. The last was the paper-thin shell of a female argonauta, which releases its eggs and allows its young to float away, just as children in a family leave home to find their own way.

The double-sunrise shells Anne mentions in Gift from the Sea are more commonly found as half shells (bottom).

As she prepared to leave the island, Anne felt that she should not take all the shells she had found. She needed to select the best one of each kind and "set it apart by itself, ringed around by space—like the island." Then it would be beautiful and "significant." She saw that her own life was lacking empty space. She had filled her life with too many people, too many activities. She hoped the shells would remind her to maintain the simplicity and selectivity of her island life.

She sent her finished manuscript to Kurt Wolff, who had founded Pantheon Books after he emigrated to the United States from Europe in 1941. When she met him, she found him warm and worldly and thought he would be the right person to publish her book. As soon as he read it, he wrote Anne, "It is a lovely and touching book—written with that scrupulous care and workmanship which distinguishes you. . . . I think you have made the case of women in this country, in our times, poignantly clear." He promised to publish the book with great care.

In 1955 *Gift from the Sea* was published. Each chapter begins with a black-and-white line drawing of a shell, and the original cover illustration is a deep blue sea revealing shells within its gentle waves.

Anne touched society's nerves with her lyrical words. The sadness was that she could not rejoice with her mother or her mother-in-law. Both women died just before her book was published, and their deaths left her distraught. Charles was away constantly, and although she sought solitude, she did not want it full-time.

Gift from the Sea has remained in print ever since its publication in 1955. In 2005 it was reissued in a fiftieth-anniversary edition, with a foreword by Anne's daughter, Reeve. For fifty years, women have found in the book answers to their many questions about juggling their roles as wife, mother, and breadwinner.

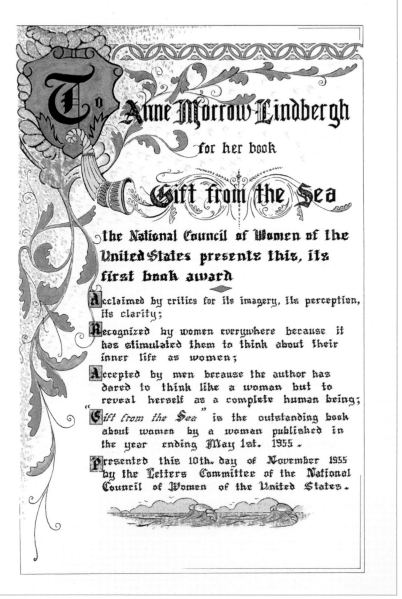

*The National Council of Women of the United States presented
Anne with this certificate in 1955 for writing Gift from the Sea.*

"What a circus act we women perform every day of our lives," Anne wrote, describing her life and theirs.

In 1953 Charles had published his book *The Spirit of St. Louis,* which Anne had helped him edit and revise. When the book won a Pulitzer Prize the following year, she expressed great pleasure about his award but also a certain amount of envy. She wrote, "I helped him write the book. I helped it to be that perfect. I know it never would have been that perfect without my help." But Charles knew. He dedicated the book to her: "To A. M. L., who will never realize how much of this book she has written."

Anne had always wanted to collect her poetry and see it published. Her dream came true in September 1956 when Pantheon published *The Unicorn and Other Poems.* Most of the reviews were positive until January 1957, when John Ciardi, poetry editor of the *Saturday Review of Literature,* called her poems "inept, jingling, slovenly, illiterate even." Readers sent hundreds of angry letters to the magazine to protest Ciardi's review and request that he be fired. The head of the magazine defended his poetry editor's right to express himself but disagreed with what he said about Anne's poetry.

Anne never got over the criticism of her poetry and published only one additional poem in the *Atlantic Monthly* at the end of the year. In 1962 she wrote another novel, *Dearly Beloved,* in which her many characters express thoughts about their own marriages while they attend a family wedding. She wrote Con that she was determined to keep her own thirty-year marriage intact: "I must accept the fact that my husband is as completely different from me as he can be." These were almost the exact words she had written when she decided to marry Charles. Then she had worried that there was a huge chasm between them. The chasm was still there.

They were very different people, but she felt they had found ways to share with each other despite the differences.

She wrote her daughter Anne in 1963, after Ansy married a young French student, "I do not really think happiness is the point of marriage. . . . Actually, I think I am just beginning to understand your father, after all these years, & he perhaps, me. (Understanding is a very different thing from the deep bond between us which has always been there.)" Because Charles was away so much, Anne had stopped trying to follow his rules, and that made her life easier.

THIRTEEN

A Solitary Life

*[I]n my father she had lost a
professional partner, as well
as a personal one.*
—Reeve Lindbergh, *Under a Wing*, 1998

In October 1965, Anne and Charles invited their family to
join them on a trip to southern Kenya in Africa. All of them accepted the invitation except Land and his wife, who said they did
not want to follow what they expected to be Charles's rigorous
schedule.

The group spent a month camping and visiting national
parks and observing animal life. Physically, it was a strenuous
trip, but Charles seemed to thrive on the hardships and was un-
fazed by "heat, flies, dust, bad roads, long hours, canned food,
ticks, and lack of washing water!" Anne wrote a friend. He had
made intricate lists for their daily activities, just as he had always
done at home and for every project he conceived.

After the African trip, Charles became concerned with environmental issues on that continent and in other countries around

138

Charles [left] *had traveled alone to Kenya in 1964 and returned with his family in 1965. His travels deepened his interest in protecting the environment.*

the world. He spent his last years, traveling and writing about conservation of the land and its wildlife. Anne shared his concern for preserving the natural world. She gave their wedding gift of Big Garden Island in Maine to the Nature Conservancy for use by the National Park Service.

As he traveled, Charles had decided they should have a small house in Vevey, Switzerland—a setting Anne loved. He built another house in Maui, Hawaii, a place he liked equally as much.

Even though Charles had told Anne not to spend so much time on her diaries, he now encouraged her to edit them for publication. He saw that she had lived through important years in the history of the country, and she should share her thoughts with the public. Anne was hesitant at first, but once she began reading her diaries, she agreed. The person she had been in those earlier years was gone. She was no longer the insecure, naive young thing she found on those pages.

Anne wrote introductions to each volume of her diaries and letters. These allowed her to explain their lives with the added wisdom and insight that the years had brought.

Her first volume was published in 1972 as *Bring Me a Unicorn: Diaries and Letters, 1922–1928. Hour of Gold, Hour of Lead* was published the following year. There were three additional volumes: *Locked Rooms and Open Doors, The Flower and the Nettle,* and *War Within and Without.* Readers felt that they "were reading about a friend," and Anne became "one of the century's most popular diarists."

In the 1970s, it was discovered that Charles had lymphoma—cancer of the lymph nodes. He was treated with radiation and chemotherapy, but these could not cure his cancer. As he grew weaker, he was hospitalized in New York. He knew he

Anne, pictured here at her writing desk in 1969, started to prepare her personal writings for publication in the late 1960s.
The first volume, Bring Me a Unicorn: Diaries and Letters, 1922–1928, *came out in 1972.*

didn't have much longer to live. Charles had chosen to die in Hawaii, in the home he had built there. He told his doctors he wanted to leave the hospital, and he signed himself out despite what they said.

Anne, Jon, Scott, and Land went with him to Hawaii. From his bed, Charles planned every detail of his funeral preparations on the island. He chose the hymns to be sung and who would dig his grave. He chose the granite stone and the words it would hold: "If I take the wings of the morning, /And dwell in the uttermost parts of the sea" from Psalm 139.

Charles Lindbergh died in Maui, Hawaii, on Monday, August 26, 1974—a little more than a week later. He had a very peaceful death, in exactly the setting he had chosen and with the service and the people he had selected.

After Charles's death, Anne returned to their small home in Connecticut. She also spent time at the chalet in Vevey, Switzerland. Anne visited her children and thirteen grandchildren in France and throughout the United States. They called her Granny Mouse. She lived more than twenty-six years without Charles. During those years, she completed the editing of her last volumes of journals in 1980, but she did not write any new books. Her daughter Reeve suggested that she had intended to write them, but that once Charles was gone, "she had lost a professional partner, as well as a personal one."

She even stopped writing in her diary as frequently as she had during the earlier years. Her letters became a substitute for her internal questioning. She was just as honest when she wrote to her children or close friends, but she stopped examining her motives and disappointments. She continued to feed the birds that visited her homes in Switzerland and Connecticut, and she collected the delicate bird feathers she found everywhere she lived.

Memorials were built to honor Charles. Anne traveled to Saint Paul, Minnesota, in 1985, to unveil a handsome statue of Charles as both boy and flier. That same year, she attended the opening of the Lindbergh air terminal in Minneapolis, Minnesota. She attended meetings of the Lindbergh Foundation, which was founded by the Explorer's Club to promote a balance between technology and conservation, and presented awards to grant recipients. In 1995 she presented the award to the queen of Thailand for her efforts to preserve the environment in her country.

Anne and Reeve shared a great deal with each other. They were both writers who understood the mysterious process of creating and the need for solitude from a busy family life. They also shared great tragedy. Both of them had young sons who had died before they were two, although their deaths were fifty years apart.

Reeve's son Jonny was almost the same age as baby Charlie had been, when one early morning in 1985, she went in to get him and found him dead in his crib. Jonny had died from a seizure related to the encephalitis, or inflammation of the brain, he had suffered earlier.

No matter how great Reeve's sense of shock and grief, her mother insisted they sit together with Jonny's body. She told her daughter she had never been able to sit with Charlie when his decayed body was found. Charles had identified the baby and had had him cremated immediately, thinking he was sparing Anne. She had needed to mourn her child and would do so as she sat with her daughter, mourning this baby's death.

When Anne suffered a stroke in January 1991, Reeve's husband, Nathaniel Tripp, designed and had built a replica of her Swiss chalet on their property in northern Vermont. That was where Anne spent her last months, with attendants and visits from her children and grandchildren. She was silent most of the time due to additional small strokes. She always kept a stack of books next to her chair and read from them all day long. Reeve came to visit Anne every evening, hoping her mother would speak to her as she talked about the day, but Anne rarely said a word.

A short time before she died, Reeve read her mother *Gift from the Sea.* Anne seemed to listen carefully, but then she grew sad. Reeve wondered if she had returned to those times on the Captiva beach when she began to write the book. She often "float[ed] in time," remembering a moment from the past, Reeve wrote in her memoir.

Anne Morrow Lindbergh died on Wednesday, February 7, 2001. Despite a heavy snowstorm, her son Jon was able to reach Vermont just before her death. Reeve and Jon sat with their mother on Tuesday, while she was still alive. The next morning, Anne stopped breathing just as they came into her cottage. The two of them and all her caregivers came to sit with her and say their farewells. Birds filled the snowy branches of the tree outside her window. Reeve was certain there were no birds in the trees the day before Anne died. But on that day, chickadees, juncos, and a single blue jay had come to pay their respects.

Epilogue

Anne's brother Dwight died in 1976, shortly after Charles's death. He had been well after his treatment for schizophrenia and had received a Ph.D in history. He taught history for many years. Anne remained close to her sister Con until Con died in 1995.

The Lindbergh children also remain close to one another, even though they live far apart. Reeve is a well-known writer, and she was kind and honest with her comments when I asked for her help. She has been called the shepherd of the family. Jon is a consultant with organizations growing foods, such as cranberry farming in Chile. Land works on environmental issues in Montana and other Western states. Scott lives in Brazil after spending many years in France, where he studied primates. Ansy was a talented writer and musician. She died of melanoma in 1993, when she was only fifty-three years old.

Author's Note

I have admired Anne Morrow Lindbergh since I was a young and inexperienced mother many years ago. Her *Gift from the Sea* became as important to me as Dr. Spock's baby book—my generation's guide to child rearing. Together, those books sat on my nightstand and grew tattered with constant searching. I, too, was torn between my duties and my need to create. Her words gave me guidance and inspiration.

I was thrilled to have this chance to write her biography. But as soon as I mentioned I was writing about Anne Morrow Lindbergh, friends uttered negative comments. "Oh, she was married to a Nazi," and "Charles Lindbergh was anti-Semitic; so was his wife." They called her a "terrible spoiled brat," or said that she was a "meek woman, dominated by her demanding husband." Or they simply asked, "Why write about *her?*"

I needed to find out who Anne Morrow Lindbergh really was, so that I could answer such questions. In preparation for this biography I read her books on flying, five volumes of published journals, her poetry, and many books about her. I reread *Gift from the Sea* to learn whether it was still as meaningful to me. This time I could appreciate her poetic language, when earlier I was looking only for answers. I also discovered that all of her books contain a spiritual philosophy about relationships and a clear view of the natural world, which are as strong today as they were when she wrote them. Whenever I was lost, I could revisit her words and find my way.

Anne Morrow Lindbergh led a privileged life. Her family had servants while she was growing up. After her marriage, she and Charles also could afford servants. Yet she knew how to work hard when it was necessary, beginning with her honeymoon on the *Mouette*. She helped Charles keep the ship clean, scrubbing it down daily. She cooked the meals and kept order in the galley. She also learned to use the ship's tools so that she could help Charles navigate.

She went on to become his radio operator and a pilot in her own right, and she accompanied her husband on many trips to map routes for the airlines. She packed up and made new homes for Charles and their children whenever it was necessary. In later years, though, she found she needed to stop traveling and seek peace with her books, her music, and her friends.

Their daughter, Reeve, said that she and her siblings were taught to respect all people. Her parents never made negative comments about any group and never told the ethnic jokes that she heard in other people's homes. Were her parents anti-Semitic? Certainly Anne was not. Charles insisted he was not, even though his words or actions were often construed as such.

Charles may have been duped by the Germans' superiority in aviation. He may have minimized the horrors of the Holocaust. "We were both very blind, especially in the beginning, to the worst evils of the Nazi system," Anne wrote late in life.

There is no question that Anne and Charles Lindbergh were controversial in their ideas and in their unique explorations of the world. Their lives were as intertwined as vines stretching to the sun. I quickly learned that I couldn't write about Anne without writing about Charles.

I discovered that Charles Lindbergh was a complex, determined man, with "terrific drive," according to Anne. He told his children how to live their lives. He wrote lists of tasks for himself, for Anne, and for the children. He nudged Anne to take writing assignments, always to write the next book, even finally to edit her diaries. He called her the "great writer" in the family despite her denials.

Charles built homes all over the world for Anne and his family. In 2003 it came out that in the 1950s, he had fathered a second family in Germany. Perhaps, when he stopped building homes for his first family, he needed to continue building homes and writing lists for another family.

Anne most likely never knew about his German family. She accepted his many foibles in their forty-five years together. I think that she would have accepted his second family, as she had accepted his other imperfections.

At first I thought I had to excuse or explain many of their actions, but then I realized that wasn't necessary. I could tell Anne's story and show where she and Charles came together and grew apart. Each reader would be free to interpret or question the way she lived her life. Anne Morrow Lindbergh's words continue to be beacons of wisdom for me.

Important Dates

June 22, 1906   Anne Morrow Lindbergh is born in Englewood, New Jersey.

1919   She attends Miss Chapin's School, New York City.

September 1924   She attends Smith College.

December 1927   She travels to Mexico and meets Charles Lindbergh.

May 1928   She graduates from Smith College.

May 27, 1929   She marries Charles Lindbergh.

June 22, 1930   Charles Jr. is born.

July 1931   Anne begins flight with Charles to Japan and China. She makes her first solo flight.

March 1, 1932   Baby Charles is kidnapped.

August 16, 1932   Jon is born.

July 1933   Anne and Charles begin Atlantic survey flight.

1934   National Geographic Society awards Anne its Hubbard Gold Medal.

January 2, 1935   The kidnapping trial of Bruno Hauptmann begins.

February 1935   *North to the Orient* is published. Smith College awards Anne an honorary degree.

December 21, 1935   The Lindberghs leave the United States.

May 12, 1937   Land is born in London.

1938   The Lindberghs move to Illiec Island, France. *Listen! the Wind* is published.

1939	The family returns to the United States as WWII begins in Europe.
1940	Harcourt publishes *The Wave of the Future.*
October 2, 1940	Anne Spencer is born.
August 13, 1942	Scott is born.
October 2, 1945	Reeve is born.
1955	Pantheon publishes *Gift from the Sea.*
September 1956	*The Unicorn and Other Poems* is published.
1962	Anne's novel, *Dearly Beloved*, is published.
1972	*Bring Me A Unicorn: Diaries and Letters 1922–1928* is published.
1973	*Hour of Gold, Hour of Lead: Diaries and Letters 1929–1932* is published.
1974	*Locked Rooms and Open Doors: Diaries and Letters 1933–1935* is published.
August 26, 1974	Charles Lindbergh dies.
1976	*Flower and Nettle: Diaries and Letters 1936–1939* is published.
1980	*War Within and Without: Diaries and Letters 1939–1944* is published.
1991	Anne suffers small strokes.
May 1999	Anne moves to Vermont.
February 7, 2001	Anne Morrow Lindbergh dies at the age of 94.

Sources

7   A. Scott Berg, *Lindbergh* (New York: G. P. Putnam's Sons, 1998), 184.
Harold Nicolson, *Dwight Morrow* (New York: Harcourt, Brace and Company, 1935), 163.
Berg, 183.
Anne Morrow Lindbergh, *Bring Me a Unicorn* (New York: Harcourt Brace Jovanovich, 1971), xx.

11   Berg, 184.

12   Anne Morrow Lindbergh, *Bring*, 5.
Ibid., 7.

13   Ibid., 22.

15   Ibid., 47.

16   Anne Morrow Lindbergh, "Caprice," *Smith College Monthly*, 1926.
Anne Morrow Lindbergh, *Bring*, 60.

17   Ibid., 73.

18   Ibid. *Bring*, 87.

20–21   Ibid., 81.

21   Ibid., 82.
Ibid.

22   Anne Morrow Lindbergh, *Bring*, 87.
Ibid., 89.

23   Ibid., 100.

24   Ibid., 103.

27   Ibid., 124–125.
Ibid., 145.

28   Ibid., 146.
Ibid., 167.

29   Ibid., 172.
Ibid.

30   Anne Morrow Lindbergh, *Hour of Gold, Hour of Lead* (New York: Harcourt Brace Jovanovich, 1973), 3.

Anne Morrow Lindbergh, *Bring*, 175.
Ibid.

31   Ibid.
Ibid., 179.
Ibid., 180.
Ibid., 181.

32   Ibid., 185.
Ibid., 191.

33   Ibid., 194.

34   Ibid., 195.
Ibid., 196.
Ibid., 202.

35   Ibid., 205.
Susan Hertog, *Anne Morrow Lindbergh: Her Life* (New York: Anchor Books Random House, Inc., 1999), 79.
Anne Morrow Lindbergh, *Bring*, 206.

36   Ibid.
Ibid., 207.

37   Ibid., 216.
Ibid., 217.
Ibid., 219.

37–38   Ibid., 224–225.

38   Ibid.
Ibid., 228.

39   Ibid.
Anne Morrow Lindbergh, *Hour*, 3.
Ibid.
Ibid., 23.

40   Berg, 584.

41   Anne Morrow Lindbergh, *Hour*, 19.

42   Ibid.
Ibid., 20.
Hertog, 93.

43   Anne Morrow Lindberg, *War Within and Without* (New York: Harcourt Brace Jovanovich, 1980), p. xv.

44 Hertog, 103.
45 Anne Morrow Lindbergh,
    Hour, 41.
    Hertog, 109.
47 Anne Morrow Lindbergh, *War,*
    xv.
    Anne Morrow Lindbergh,
    Hour, 48.
    Ibid., 50.
49 Anne Morrow Lindbergh, *War,*
    11.
50 Anne Morrow Lindbergh,
    Hour, 11.
    Ibid., 70.
    Ibid., 105.
51 Ibid., 118.
52 Ibid., 10.
55 Ibid., 211.
    Hertog, 133.
    Anne Morrow Lindbergh,
    Hour, 138.
56 Dorothy Herrmann, A*nne
    Morrow Lindbergh: A Gift for
    Life* (New York: Ticknor and
    Fields, 1993), 70.
    Anne Morrow Lindbergh,
    Hour, 147.
    Ibid.
57–58 Ibid., 162.
58 Ibid., 11.
59 Ibid., 168.
61 Ibid., 201.
    Ibid.
63 Berg, 240.
    Anne Morrow Lindbergh,
    Hour, 211.
    Berg, 242.
64 Anne Morrow Lindbergh,
    Hour, 231.
65 Berg, 255.
66 Ibid., 262.
69 Anne Morrow Lindbergh,
    Hour, 302.

70 Ibid.
71 Ibid., 303.
    Ibid., 321.
    Ibid., 320.
73 Anne Morrow Lindbergh,
    Listen! the Wind (New York:
    Harcourt, Brace and Company,
    1938), 148.
    Anne Morrow Lindbergh,
    Locked Rooms and Open Doors
    (New York: Harcourt, Brace
    and Company, 1974), 46.
74 Ibid., 71.
    Ibid., 80.
    Ibid., 105.
75 Ibid., 107.
    Ibid.
76 Ibid., 113.
77 Ibid., 120.
    Ibid., 122.
78 Ibid., 129.
80 Anne Morrow Lindbergh,
    Listen!, 216.
    Ibid., 217.
    Ibid.
    Hertog, 239.
    Anne Morrow Lindbergh,
    Locked, xxvi.
83 Ibid., 247.
84 Hertog, 252.
84–85 Anne Morrow Lindbergh,
    Locked, 229.
87 Ibid., 247.
    Hertog, 258.
88 Anne Morrow Lindbergh,
    Locked, 245.
    Ibid., 268.
89 Hertog, 273.
    Ibid.
90 Anne Morrow Lindbergh, *The
    Flower and the Nettle* (New
    York: Harcourt Brace, and
    Company, 1976), p. xi.

91   Anne Morrow Lindbergh, *Locked*, 336.

92   Herrmann, 139.

93   Anne Morrow Lindbergh, *Flower*, 30.

        Ibid., 33.

95   Berg, 361.

96   Anne Morrow Lindbergh, *Flower*, 198.

        Ibid., 142.

96–97   Ibid. 146.

98   Ibid., 198.

        Ibid., 197.

        Ibid., x.

99   Ibid., xi.

100   Ibid., 84.

        Herrmann, 202.

101   Anne Morrow Lindbergh, *Flower*, xvi.

101–102 Ibid.

102   Ibid.

        Hertog, 337.

103   Anne Morrow Lindbergh, *Flower*, 391.

        Hertog, 342.

        Ibid.

104   Anne Morrow Lindbergh, *Flower*, 401.

        Ibid., 408.

        Ibid.

        Ibid., 422.

105   Ibid., 470.

        Ibid., 406.

106   Berg, 386.

        Ibid., 479.

        Anne Morrow Lindbergh, *Flower*, 498.

107   Anne Morrow Lindbergh, *War*, 35.

109   Hertog, 358.

        Anne Morrow Lindbergh, *War*, 33.

        Ibid.

        Ibid., 23.

        Ibid.

110   Ibid., 45.

113   Ibid., 88–89.

        Ibid., 98.

        Berg, 405.

114   Ibid., 406.

        Ibid., 407.

115   Ibid., 425.

        Ibid., 426.

116   Herrmann, 223.

        Ibid., 322.

117   Anne Morrow Lindbergh, *War*, 248.

119   Anne Morrow Lindbergh, *War*, 449.

        Ibid., 236.

120   Ibid.

        Ibid.

121   Ibid., 262.

        Ibid., 263.

        Ibid., 275.

122   Ibid., 306.

        Ibid., 297.

123   Ibid., 382.

124   Ibid., 344–345.

        Ibid., 338.

        Ibid., 348.

        Antoine de Saint-Exupéry, *The Little Prince* (New York: Harcourt Brace and Company, 1971), 73.

        Anne Morrow Lindbergh, *War*, 360–361.

124–125 Ibid., 386.

125   Ibid.

126   Ibid., 392.

        Ibid., 412.

        Ibid., 419.

128   Ibid., 446.

        Ibid., 449.

        Ibid., 440.

128–129 Ibid., 447.

129   Reeve Lindbergh, *Under a Wing: A Memoir* (New York: Simon and Schuster, 1998), 61.

131 Anne Morrow Lindbergh, "Airliner to Europe: Notes from a Passenger's Diary," *Harper's Magazine*, September 1948, 43–44. Anne Morrow Lindbergh, "The Flame of Europe," *Reader's Digest*, January 1948, 141.

132 Anne Morrow Lindbergh, *Gift from the Sea* (New York: Pantheon, 1955), 26.

133 Ibid., 80.

134 Ibid., 114. Ibid. Berg, 491.

136 Ibid. Ibid., 490.

Ibid., 497. Anne Morrow Lindbergh, *Gift*, 26. Berg, 490. Ibid., 500.

137 Ibid., 515.

138 Reeve Lindbergh, *Under a Wing*, 217. Berg, 524.

140 Ibid., 547.

141 Reeve Lindbergh, *Under a Wing*, 217.

143 Reeve Lindbergh, *No More Words: A Journal of My Mother* (New York: Simon and Schuster, 2001), 159.

146–147 Berg, 469.

147 Ibid., 491.

Selected Bibliography

Berg, A. Scott. *Lindbergh*. New York: G. P. Putnam's Sons, 1998.

Herrmann, Dorothy. *Anne Morrow Lindbergh: A Gift for Life*. New York: Ticknor and Fields Houghton Mifflin Co., 1993.

Hertog, Susan. *Anne Morrow Lindbergh: Her Life*. New York: Anchor Books Random House, Inc., 1999.

Lindbergh, Anne Morrow. *Bring Me A Unicorn*. New York: Harcourt Brace Jovanovich, 1971.

———. *The Flower and the Nettle*. New York: Harcourt, Brace and Company, 1976.

———. *Gift from the Sea*. New York: Pantheon, 1955.

———. *Hour of Gold, Hour of Lead*. New York: Harcourt Brace Jovanovich, 1973.

———. *Listen! The Wind*. New York: Harcourt, Brace and Company, 1938.

———. *Locked Rooms and Open Doors*. A Helen and Kurt Wolff Book. New York: Harcourt, Brace and Company, 1974.

———. *North to the Orient*. New York: Harcourt, Brace and Company, 1935.

———. *The Unicorn and Other Poems*. New York: Vintage Books, 1972.

———. *War Within and Without*. New York: Harcourt Brace Jovanovich, 1980.

Lindbergh, Reeve. *No More Words: A Journal of My Mother*. New York: Simon and Schuster, 2001.

———. *Under a Wing: A Memoir*. New York: Simon and Schuster, 1998.

Nicolson, Harold. *Dwight Morrow*. New York: Harcourt, Brace and Company, 1935.

Saint-Exupéry, Antoine de. *The Little Prince*. New York: Harcourt Brace and Company, 1971.

Shirer, William L. *The Rise and Fall of the Third Reich: A History of Nazi Germany*. New York: Simon and Schuster, 1960.

Vaughan, David Kirk. *Anne Morrow Lindbergh*. Boston: Twayne Publishers, 1988.

Articles

Lindbergh, Anne Morrow. "Airliner to Europe: Notes from a Passenger's Diary." *Harper's Magazine*, September 1948, 43–47.

———. "The Flame of Europe." *Reader's Digest* 52, January 1948, 141–46.

Telephone Interviews

Telephone interview with Ruth DeHovitz, the author's friend, who heard Charles Lindbergh's September 11, 1941 speech in Des Moines, Iowa, when she was a child. August 22, 2004.

Telephone interview with Reeve Lindbergh, Anne Morrow Lindbergh's daughter. October 20, 2004.

Telephone interview with Katchen Coley, whose parents, Truman and Kay Smith, were friends of the Lindberghs in Berlin. Major Smith was military attaché in Berlin during the 1930s. November 8, 2004.

Further Reading and Websites

The Charles A. and Anne Morrow Lindbergh Foundation
http://www.lindberghfoundation.org
The foundation's site contains biographies of both of them, photos, and a history of aviation as well as information about its mission to support "technological solutions to improve our environment for a sustainable future" as did Charles A. and Anne Morrow Lindbergh.

Feldman, Ruth Tenzer. *World War I.* Minneapolis: Twenty-First Century Books, 2004.

Giblin, James Cross. *Charles A. Lindbergh: A Human Hero.* New York: Clarion, 1997.

Goldstein, Margaret J. *World War II: Europe.* Minneapolis: Twenty-First Century Books, 2004.

NPR: Anne Morrow Lindbergh's Long-Lasting 'Gift.'
http://www.npr.org/templates/story/story.php?storyId=5232208
This site contains brief biographical information about Anne, along with excerpts from *Gift from the Sea*, and links to related NPR stories.

Saint-Exupéry, Antoine de. *The Little Prince.* New York: Harcourt Brace and Company, 1971.

Trial Account: Richard Hauptmann (Lindbergh Kidnapping) Trial 1935
http://www.law.umkc.edu/faculty/projects/ftrials/Hauptmann/Hauptmann.htm
This site is a University of Missouri, Kansas City, Law School overview of the trial of the Lindbergh baby's kidnapper. It includes trial transcripts, newspaper accounts, photos, and more.

Williams, Barbara. *World War II: Pacific.* Minneapolis: Twenty-First Century Books, 2004.

Index

157

Photo Acknowledgments

The images in this book are used with the permission of: Lindbergh Picture Collection, Manuscripts & Archives, Yale University Library, pp. 2, 6, 41, 52, 59, 60, 74, 75, 76, 86, 91, 97, 99, 101, 127, 130, 135, 139, 140; National Archives, pp. 8 (306-NT-157785c), 9 (306-NT-168624c), 24 (306-NT-172930c), 62 (306-NT-313-12); © Bettmann/CORBIS, pp. 10, 39, 111; © Underwood & Underwood/CORBIS, p. 14; Minneapolis Public Library, Minneapolis Collection, p. 19; © Lindbergh Picture Collection, Manuscripts & Archives, Yale University Library, pp. 20, 46, 48, 57, 115, 118, 120, 123; AP Photo, pp. 26, 64, 67, 77, 85; Library of Congress, p. 31 (LC-USZ62-49032); © Skyscan/CORBIS, p. 33; © Getty Images, pp. 51, 82, 102, 112; © New York Times Co./Getty Images, p. 54; National Air and Space Museum, Smithsonian Institution, p. 72; Minnesota Historical Society, p. 92; © Heinrich Hoffmann/Timepix/Time Life Pictures/Getty Images, p. 95; © Mary Evans Picture Library/Alamy, p. 108; Franklin D. Roosevelt Library, p. 117; © Pete Turner/The Image Bank/Getty Images, p. 133; Charles R. Gherman, p. 160.

Front cover: © Bettmann/CORBIS.

About the Author

 Beverly Gherman has chosen to write about artists and writers whose creations endure long after their creators' deaths. Georgia O'Keeffe was the subject of Gherman's first biography, followed by books about E. B. White, Norman Rockwell, Robert Louis Stevenson, Ansel Adams, and more. This biography about Anne Morrow Lindbergh is the latest in a line of strong complex individuals whose lives have given her an understanding of the creative process.

As a young woman, Gherman found inspiration in Lindbergh's book, *Gift from the Sea*. In doing research for this biography, she read all Lindbergh's published journals and books. They revealed how Anne Lindbergh became a partner to her husband, Charles, in the sky and in their lives together, and also how she maintained her individuality through her sensitive, poetic words.

Gherman lives in San Francisco with her husband.